HAPPY DAYS

A. A. Milne

[ZHINGOORA BOOKS]

This edition is published by
Zhingoora Books.

This book is made up from my contributions to *Punch*—a casual selection from the four hundred or so which have appeared in the last nine years. It is offered to the American public as a sample of that *Punch* humour (and perhaps, therefore, British humour) which Americans so often profess not to understand. According to whether they like it or do not like it, I hope they will consider it a representative or an unrepresentative sample.

A.A.M.

CONTENTS

MARGERY

MARGERY

I. HER SOCK

I

When Margery was three months old I wrote a letter to her mother:

Dear Madam,—If you have a copy in Class D at 1/10d. net, I shall be glad to hear from you.I am,The Baby's Uncle.

On Tuesday I got an answer by the morning post:

Dear Sir,—In reply to yours: How dare you insult my child? She is in Class A1, priceless and bought in by the owner. Four months old (and two days) on Christmas Day. Fancy!I am,The Baby's Mother.

Margery had been getting into an expensive way of celebrating her birthday every week. Hitherto I had ignored it. But now I wrote:

Dear Madam,—Automatically your baby should be in Class D by now. I cannot understand why it is not so. Perhaps I shall hear from you later on with regard to this. Meanwhile I think that the extraordinary coincidence (all but two days) of the baby's birthday with Christmas Day calls for some recognition on my part. What would Margery like? You, who are in constant communication with her, should be able to tell me. I hear coral necklaces well spoken of. What do you think? I remember reading once of a robber who "killed a little baby for the coral on its neck"—which shows at any rate that they are worn. Do you know how coral reefs are made? It is a most fascinating business.Then there is a silver mug to be considered. The only thing you can drink out of a mug is beer; yet it is a popular present. Perhaps you, with your (supposed) greater knowledge of babies, will explain this.Meanwhile, I am,The Baby's Uncle.P.S.—Which is a much finer thing than a mother.

To which her mother:

My Dear Boy,—It is too sweet of you to say you would like to get Baby something. No, I don't know how coral reefs are made, and don't want to. I think it is wicked of you to talk like that; I'm sure I shan't dare let her wear anything valuable now. And I don't think she really wants a mug. I'm sure I don't know what she does want, except to see her uncle (There!) but it ought to be something that she'll value when she grows up. And of course we could keep it for her in the meantime.Her Father has smoked his last cigar to-day. Isn't it awful? I have forbidden him to waste his money on any more, but he says he must give me 500 for a Christmas present. If he does, I shall give him that sideboard that I want so badly, and then we shall both go to prison together. You will look after Baby, won't you?I am,The Baby's Mother.P.S.—Which she isn't proud, but does think it's a little bit classier than an uncle.

And so finally, I:

Dear Child,—I've thought of the very thing.I am,The Baby's Uncle.

That ends Chapter I. Here we go on to

II

Chapter II finds me in the Toy Department of the Stores. "I want," I said, "a present for a child."

"Yes, sir. About how old?"

"It must be quite new," I said sternly. "Don't be silly. Oh, I see; well, the child is only a baby."

"Ah, yes. Now here—if it's at all fond of animals——"

"I say, you mustn't call it 'IT.' I get in an awful row if I do. Of course, I suppose it's all right for you, only—well, be careful, won't you?"

The attendant promised, and asked whether the child was a boy or girl.

"And had you thought of anything for the little girl?"

"Well, yes. I had rather thought of a sideboard."

"I beg your pardon?"

"A sideboard."

"The Sideboard Department is upstairs. Was there anything else for the little girl?"

"Well, a box of cigars. Rather full, and if you have any——"

"The Cigar Department is on the ground floor."

"But your Lord Chamberlain told me I was to come here if I wanted a present for a child."

"If you require anything in the toy line——"

"Yes, but what good are toys to a baby of four months? Do be reasonable."

"What was it you suggested? A sideboard and a cigar?"

"That was my idea. It may not be the best possible, but at least it is better than perfectly useless toys. You can always blow smoke in its face, or bump its head against the sideboard. *Experto crede*, if you have the Latin."

Whereupon with great dignity I made my way to the lift.

In the Sideboard Department I said: "I want a sideboard for a little girl of four months, and please don't call her 'IT.' I nearly had a row with one of your downstairs staff about that."

"I will try to be careful about that, Sir," he replied. "What sort of a one?"

"Blue eyes and not much hair, and really rather a sweet smile.... Was that what you wanted to know?"

"Thank you, Sir. But I meant, what sort of a sideboard?"

I took him confidentially by the arm.

"Look here," I said, "you know how, when one is carrying a baby about, one bumps its head at all the corners? Well, not too much of that. The mothers don't really like it, you know. They smile at the time, but.... Well, not too many corners.... Yes, I like that very much. No, I won't take it with me."

The attendant wrote out the bill.

"Number, Sir?"

"She's the first. That's why I'm so nervous. I've never bought a sideboard for a child before.

"Your Stores number, I mean, Sir."

"I haven't got one. Is it necessary?"

"Must have a number, Sir."

"Then I'll think of a nice one for you.... Let's see—12345, how does that strike you?"

"And the name?"

"Oh, I can't tell you that. You must look that up for yourself. Good-day."

Downstairs I bought some cigars.

"For a little girl of four months," I said, "and she likes them rather full. Please don't argue with me. All your men chatter so."

"I must," said the attendant. "It's like this. If she is only four months, she is obviously little. Your observation is therefore tautological."

"As a matter of fact," I said hotly, "she is rather big for four months."

"Then it was a lie."

"Look here, you give me those cigars, and don't talk so much. I've already had words with your Master of the Sideboards and your Under-Secretary for the Toy Department.... Thank you. If you would kindly send them."

III

So there it is. I have given the spirit rather than the actual letter, of what happened at the Stores. But that the things have been ordered there is no doubt. And when Margery wakes up on Christmas Day to find a sideboard and a box of cigars in her sock I hope she will remember that she has chiefly her mother to thank for it.

II. HOW WE PLAY THE PIANOLA

[FOREWORD. Margery wishes me to publish the following correspondence, which has recently passed between us. It occurs to me that the name under which I appear in it may perhaps need explanation. I hate explanations, but here it is.

When Margery was eight months old, she was taught to call me "Uncle." I must suppose that at this time I was always giving her things—things she really wanted, such as boot-laces, the best china, evening papers and so on—which had been withheld by those in authority. Later on, these persons came round to my way of thinking, and gave her, if not the best china, at any rate cake and bread-and-butter. Naturally their offerings, being appreciated at last, were greeted with the familiar cry of "Uncle," "No, dear, not 'Uncle,' 'Thank-you,'" came the correction.]

I

Dear Thankyou,—I've some wonderful news for you! Guess what it is; but no, you never will. Well, I'll tell you. I can walk! Really and really.It is most awfully interesting. You put one foot out to the right, and then you bring the left after it. That's one walk, and I have done seven altogether. You have to keep your hands out in front of you, so as to balance properly. That's all the rules—the rest is just knack. I got it quite suddenly. It is such fun; I wake up about five every morning now, thinking of it.Of course I fall down now and then. You see, I'm only beginning. When I fall, Mother comes and picks me up. That reminds me, I don't want you to call me "Baby" any more now I can walk. Babies can't walk, they just get carried about and put in perambulators. I was given a lot of names a long time ago, but I forget what they were. I think one was rather silly, like

Margery, but I have never had it used lately. Mother always calls me O.D. now.Good-bye. Write directly you get this.Your loving,O.D.

II

My Dear O.D.,—I was so glad to get your letter, because I was just going to write to you. What do you think? No, you'll never guess— shall I tell you?—no—yes—no; well, I've bought a pianola!It's really rather difficult to play it properly. I know people like Paderewski and—I can only think of Paderewski for the moment, I know that sort of person doesn't think much of the pianola artist; but they are quite wrong about it all. The mechanical agility with the fingers is nothing, the soul is everything. Now you can get the soul, the *con molto expressione* feeling, just as well in the pianola as in the piano. Of course you have to keep a sharp eye on the music. Some people roll it off just like a barrel-organ; but when I see *Allegro* or *Andante* or anything of that kind on the score, I'm on it like a bird.No time for more now, as I've just got a new lot of music in.Your loving,Thankyou.P.S.—When are you coming to hear me play? I did "Mumbling Mose" just now, with one hand and lots of soul.(Signed) Paderewski.P.P.S.—I am glad you can walk.

III

Dear Thankyou,—I am rather upset about my walking. You remember I told you I had done seven in my last? Well, this morning I couldn't do a single one! Well, I did do one, as a matter of fact, but I suppose some people would say it didn't count, because I fell down directly after, though I don't see that that matters,—do you, Thankyou? But even with that one it was only one, and yet I know I did seven the day before. I wonder why it is. I do it the right way, I'm sure, and I keep my hands out so as to balance, so perhaps it's the shoes that are wrong. I must ask Mother to get me a new pair, and tell the man they're for walks.Now do write me a nice long letter, Thankyou, because I feel very miserable about this. It is right, isn't it, when you have the right leg out, only to bring the left one just up to it, and not beyond? And does it matter which foot you start with? Let me know quickly, because Father is coming home to-morrow and I want to show him.Your loving,O.D.P.S.—I am glad you like your pianola.

IV

Dear O.D.,—Very glad to get yours. If you really want a long letter, you shall have one; only I warn you that if once I begin nothing less than any earthquake can stop me. Well, first, then, I played the Merry Widow Waltz yesterday to Mrs. Polacca, who is a great authority on music, and in with all the Queen's Hall set, and she said that my touch reminded her of—I've forgotten the man's name now, which is rather sickening, because it spoils the story a bit, but he was one of the real tiptoppers who makes hundreds a week, and well, that was the sort of man I reminded her of. If I can do that with a waltz, it stands to reason that with something classic there'd be no holding me. I think I shall give a recital. Tickets 10/6d. No free seats. No emergency exit. It is a great mistake to have an emergency exit at a recital.

(Three pages omitted.)

Really, O.D., you must hear me doing the double F in the Boston Cake Walk to get me at my best. You've heard Kubelik on the violin? Well, it's not a bit like that, and yet there's just the something which links great artists together, no matter what their medium of expression.Your loving,Thankyou.P.S.—Glad you're getting on so well with your walking.

V

Dearest Thankyou,—Hooray, hooray, hooray—I did twenty-five walks to-day! Father counted. He says my style reminds him of "*Cancer Vulgaris*" rather. How many times can he do it? Not twenty-five on the third day, I'm sure.Isn't it splendid of me? I see now where I was wrong yesterday. I got the knack again suddenly this morning, and I'm all right now. To-morrow I shall walk round the table. It is a longish way and there are four turns, which I am not sure about. How do you turn? I suppose you put the right hand out?Your very loving,O.D.

VI

Dear O.D.,—I am rather hurt by your letters. I have written several times to tell you all about my new pianola, and you don't seem to take any interest at all. I was going to have told you this time that the man in the flat below had sent me a note, just as if it had been a real piano. He says he doesn't mind my playing all day, so long as I don't start before eight in the morning, as he is in his bath then, and in listening to the music quite forgets to come out sometimes, which I can see might be very awkward.Write to yours affectionately,Thankyou.

VII

Darling Thankyou,—I am so sorry, dear, and I will come and hear your pianola to-morrow, and I think it lovely, and you must be clever to play it so well; but you musn't be angry with me because I am so taken up with my walking. You see, it is all so new to me. I feel as though I want everybody to know all about it.Your pianola must be lovely, Thankyou. Dear Thankyou, could you, do you think, put all the letters we wrote to each other about my walking in some book, so that other people would know how to do it the way I do? You might call it "Letters on Walking," or "How to Walk," or—but you could get a better title than I could. Do! Your very loving, O.D.P.S.— I'm so glad about the pianola and do you mind if I just tell you that I did walk round the table, corners and all?

VIII

Dearest O.D.,—Right you are. I will think of a good title. Your loving, Thankyou.

III. THE KNIGHT OF THE CHIMNEY-PIECE

We don't know his real name, but we have decided to call him "Arthur" ("Sir Arthur," I suppose he would be). He stands in bronze upon the chimney-piece, and in his right hand is a javelin; this makes him a very dangerous person. Opposite him, but behind the clock (Coward!), stands the other fellow, similarly armed. Most people imagine that the two are fighting for the hand of the lady on the clock, and they aver that they can hear her heart beating with the excitement of it; but, to let you into the secret, the other fellow doesn't come into the story at all. Only Margery and I know the true story. I think I told it to her one night when she wouldn't go to sleep—or perhaps she told it to me.

The best of this tale (I say it as the possible author) is that it is modern. It were easy to have invented something more in keeping with the knight's armour, but we had to remember that this was the twentieth century, and that here in this twentieth century was Sir Arthur on the chimney-piece, with his javelin drawn back. For whom is he waiting?

"It all began," I said, "a year ago, when Sir Arthur became a member of the South African Chartered Incorporated Co-operative Stores Society Limited Ten per cents at Par (Men only). He wasn't exactly a real member, having been elected under Rule Two for meritorious performances, Rule One being that this club shall be called what I said just now; but for nearly a year he enjoyed all the privileges of membership, including those of paying a large entrance fee and a still larger subscription. At the end of a year, however, a dreadful thing happened. They made a Third Rule; to wit, that no member should go to sleep on the billiard table.

"Of course, Sir Arthur having only got in under Rule Two, had to resign. He had, as I have said, paid his entrance fee, and (as it happened) his second year's subscription in advance. Naturally he was annoyed....

"And that, in fact, is why he stands on the chimney-piece with his javelin drawn back. He is waiting for the Secretary. Sir Arthur is considered to be a good shot, and the Secretary wants all the flowers to be white."

At this point Margery said her best word, "Gorky," which means, "A thousand thanks for the verisimilitude of your charming and interesting story, but is not the love element a trifle weak?" (Margery is a true woman.)

"We must leave something to the imagination," I pleaded. "The Secretary no doubt had a delightful niece, and Sir Arthur's hopeless passion for her, after he had hit her uncle in a vital spot, would be the basis of a most powerful situation."

Margery said "Gorky" again, which, as I have explained, means, "Are such distressing situations within the province of the Highest Art?"

When Margery says "Gorky" twice in one night, it is useless to argue. I gave in at once. "Butter," I said, "placed upon the haft of the javelin, would make it slip, and put him off his shot. He would miss the Secretary and marry the niece." So we put a good deal of butter on Sir Arthur, and for the moment the Secretary is safe. I don't know if we shall be able to keep it there; but in case jam does as well, Margery has promised to stroke him every day.

However, I anticipate. As soon as the secretarial life was saved, Margery said "Agga," which is as it were, "*Encore*," or "*Bis*," so that I have her permission to tell you that story all over again. Instead I will give you the tragedy of George, the other fellow (no knight he), as she told it to me afterwards.

"George was quite a different man from Sir Arthur. So far from being elected to anything under Rule Two, he got blackballed for the North London Toilet Club. Opinions differed as to why this happened; some said that it was his personal unpopularity (he had previously been up, without success, for the membership of the local Ratepayers Association) others (among them the Proprietor), that his hair grew too quickly. Anyhow, it was a great shock to George, and they had to have a man in to break it to him. (It's always the way when you have a man in.)

"George was stricken to the heart. This last blow was too much for what had always been a proud nature. He decided to emigrate. Accordingly he left home, and moved to Islington. Whether he is still there or not I cannot say; but a card with that postmark reached his niece only this week. It was unsigned, and bore on the space reserved for inland communications these words: 'The old, old wish—A Merry Christmas and a Happy New Year.'"

"But what about the javelin?" I asked Margery. (This fellow had a javelin too, you remember.)

"Gorky," said Margery for the third time, which means——

Well, upon my word, I don't know what it means. But it would explain it all.

Meanwhile Sir Arthur (he was in my story, you know) is still waiting for the Secretary. In case the butter gives out, have I mentioned that the Secretary wants *all* the flowers to be white?

IV. THE ART OF CONVERSATION

"In conversation," said somebody (I think it was my grandfather), "there should always be a give and take. The ball must be kept rolling." If he had ever had a niece two years old, I don't think he would have bothered.

"What's 'at?" said Margery, pointing suddenly.

"That," I said, stroking it, "is dear uncle's nose."

"What's 'at?"

"Take your finger away. Ah, yes, that is dear uncle's eye. The left one."

"Dear uncle's left one," said Margery thoughtfully. "What's it doing?"

"Thinking."

"What's finking?"

"What dear uncle does every afternoon after lunch."

"What's lunch?"

"Eggs, sardines, macaroons—everything."

With a great effort Margery resisted the temptation to ask what "everything" was (a difficult question), and made a statement of her own.

"Santa Claus bring Margie a balloon from Daddy," she announced.

"A balloon! How jolly!" I said with interest. "What sort are you having? One of those semi-detached ones with the gas laid on, or the pink ones with a velvet collar?"

"Down chimney," said Margery.

"Oh, that kind. Do you think—I mean, isn't it rather——"

"Tell Margie a story about a balloon."

"Bother," I murmured.

"What's bovver?"

"Bother is what you say when relations ask you to tell them a story about a balloon. It means, 'But for the fact that we both have the Montmorency blood in our veins, I should be compelled to decline your kind invitation, all the stories I know about balloons being stiff 'uns.' It also means, 'Instead of talking about balloons, won't you sing me a little song?'"

"Nope," said Margery.

"Bother, she's forgotten her music."

"What did you say, uncle dear; what did you say?"

I sighed and began.

"Once upon a time there was a balloon, a dear little toy balloon, and—and——"

"What's 'at?" asked Margery, making a dab at my chest. "What's 'at, uncle dear?"

"That," I said, "is a button. More particularly a red waistcoat button. More particularly still, my top red waistcoat button."

"What's 'at?" she asked, going down one.

"That is a button. Description: second red waistcoat. Parents living: both. Infectious diseases: scarlet fever slightly once."

"What's 'at?"

"That's a—ah, yes, a button. The third. A good little chap, but not so chubby as his brothers. He couldn't go down to Margate with them last year, and so, of course—Well, as I was saying, there was once a balloon, and——"

"What's a-a-'at?" said Margery, bending forward suddenly and kissing it.

"Look here, you've jolly well got to enclose a stamped addressed envelope with the next question. As a matter of fact, though you won't believe me, that again is a button."

"What's 'at?" asked Margery, digging at the fifth button.

"Owing to extreme pressure on space," I began.... "Thank you. That also is a button. Its responsibility is greater than that of its brethren. The crash may come at any moment. Luckily it has booked its passage to the—where was I? Oh yes—well, this balloon——"

"What's 'at?" said Margery, pointing to the last one.

"I must have written notice of that question. I can't tell you offhand."

"What's 'at, uncle dear?"

"Well, I don't know, Margie. It looks something like a collar stud, only somehow you wouldn't expect to find a collar stud there. Of course it may have slipped.... Or could it be one of those red beads, do you think?... N-no—no, it isn't a bead.... And it isn't a raspberry, because this is the wrong week for raspberries. Of course it might be a—By Jove, I've got it! It's a button."

I gave the sort of war-whoop with which one announces these discoveries, and Margery whooped too.

"A button," she cried. "A dear little button!" She thought for a moment. "What's a button?"

This was ridiculous.

"You don't mean to say," I reproached her, "that I've got to tell you now what a button is. That," I added severely, pointing to the top of my waistcoat, "is a button."

"What's 'at?" said Margery, pointing to the next one.

I looked at her in horror. Then I began to talk very quickly. "There was once a balloon," I said rapidly, "a dear little boy balloon—I mean toy balloon, and this balloon was a jolly little balloon just two minutes old, and he wasn't always asking silly questions, and when he fell down and exploded himself they used to wring him out and say, 'Come, come now, be a little airship about it,' and so——"

"What's 'at?" asked Margery, pointing to the top button.

There was only one way out of it. I began to sing a carol in a very shrill voice.

All the artist rose in Margery.

"Don't sing," she said hurriedly; "Margie sing. What shall Margie sing, uncle?"

Before I could suggest anything she was off. It was a scandalous song. She began by announcing that she wanted to be among the boys, and (anticipating my objections) assured me that it was no good kicking up a noise, because it was no fun going out when there weren't anyboys about, you were so lonely-onely-onely....

Here the tune became undecided; and, a chance word recalling another context to her mind, she drifted suddenly into a hymn, and sang it with the same religious fervour as she had sung the other, her fair head flung back, and her hazel eyes gazing into Heaven....

I listened carefully. This was a bit I didn't recognise.... The tune wavered for a moment ... and out of it these words emerged triumphant—

"Talk of me to the boys you meet,Remember me kindly to Regent Street,And give them my love in the——"

"What's 'at, uncle?"

"That," I said, stroking it, "is dear uncle's nose."

"What's——"

By the way, would you like it all over again? No? Oh, very well.

V. AFTERNOON SLEEP

[*"In the afternoon they came unto a landIn which it seemed always afternoon."*]

I am like Napoleon in that I can go to sleep at any moment; I am unlike him (I believe) in that I am always doing so. One makes no apology for doing so on Sunday afternoon; the apology indeed should come from the others, the wakeful parties....

"Uncle!"

"Margery."

"Will you come and play wiv me?"

"I'm rather busy just now," I said with closed eyes. "After tea."

"Why are you raver busy just now? My baby's only raver busy sometimes."

"Well then, you know what it's like; how important it is that one shouldn't be disturbed."

"But you *must* be beturbed when I ask you to come and play wiv me."

"Oh, well ... what shall we play at?"

"Trains," said Margery eagerly.

When we play at trains I have to be a tunnel. I don't know if you have ever been a tunnel? No; well, it's an over-rated profession.

"We won't play trains," I announced firmly, "because it's Sunday."

"Why not because it's Sunday?"

(Oh, you little pagan!)

"Hasn't Mummy told you about Sunday?"

"Oh, yes, Maud did tell me," said Margery casually. Then she gave an innocent little smile. "Oh, I called Mummy Maud," she said in pretended surprise. "I quite *fought* I was upstairs!"

I hope you follow. The manners and customs of good society must be observed on the ground floor where visitors may happen; upstairs one relaxes a little.

"Do you know," Margery went on with the air of a discoverer, "you mustn't say 'prayers' downstairs. Or 'corsets.'"

"I never do," I affirmed. "Well, anyhow I never will again."

"Why mayn't you?"

"I don't know," I said sleepily.

"Say prehaps."

"Well—*prehaps* it's because your mother tells you not to."

"Well, 'at's a *silly* fing to say," said Margery scornfully.

"It is. I'm thoroughly ashamed of it. I apologise. Good night." And I closed my eyes again....

"I fought you were going to play wiv me, Mr. Bingle," sighed Margery to herself.

"My name is not Bingle," I said, opening one eye.

"Why isn't it Bingle?"

"The story is a very long and sad one. When I wake up I will tell it to you. Good night."

"Tell it to me now."

There was no help for it.

"Once upon a time," I said rapidly, "there was a man called Bingle, Oliver Bingle, and he married a lady called Pringle. And his brother married a lady called Jingle; and his other brother married a Miss Wingle. And his cousin remained single.... That is all."

"Oh, I see," said Margery doubtfully. "Now will you play wiv me?"

How can one resist the pleading of a young child?

"All right," I said. "We'll pretend I'm a little girl, and you're my mummy, and you've just put me to bed.... Good night, mummy dear."

"Oh, but I must cover you up." She fetched a table-cloth, and a pram-cover, and *The Times*, and a handkerchief, and the cat, and a doll's what-I-mustn't-say-downstairs, and a cushion; and she covered me up and tucked me in. "'Ere, 'ere, now go to sleep, my darling," she said, and kissed me lovingly.

"Oh, Margie, you dear," I whispered.

"You called me 'Margie'!" she cried in horror.

"I meant 'Mummy.' Good night."

One, two, three seconds passed rapidly.

"It's morning," said a bright voice in my ear. "Get up."

"I'm very ill," I pleaded; "I want to stay in bed all day."

"But your dear uncle," said Margery, inventing hastily, "came last night after you were in bed, and stayed 'e night. Do you see? And he wants you to sit on him in bed and talk to him."

"Where is he? Show me the bounder."

"'Ere he is," said Margery, pointing at me.

"But look here, I can't sit on my own chest and talk to myself. I'll take the two parts if you insist, Sir Herbert, but I can't play them simultaneously. Not even Irving——"

"Why can't you play them simrulaleously?"

"Well, I can't. Margie, will you let me go to sleep?"

"Nope," said Margery, shaking her head.

"You should say, 'No thank you, revered and highly respected Uncle.'"

"No *hank* you, Mr. Cann."

"I have already informed you that my name is not Bingle and I have now to add that neither is it Cann."

"Why neiver is it Cann?"

"That isn't grammar. You should say, 'Why can it not either?'"

"Why?"

"I don't know."

"Say prehaps."

"No, I can't even say prehaps."

"Well, say I shall understand when I'm a big girl."

"You'll understand when you're a big girl, Margery," I said solemnly.

"Oh, I see."

"That's right. Now then, what about going to sleep?"

She was silent for a moment, and I thought I was safe. Then,

"Uncle, just tell me—why was 'at little boy crying vis morning?"

"Which little boy?"

"Ve one in 'e road."

"Oh, that one. Well, he was crying because his Uncle hadn't had any sleep all night, and when he tried to go to sleep in the afternoon——"

"Say prehaps again."

My first rejected contribution! I sighed and had another shot. "Well, then," I said gallantly, "it must have been because he hadn't got a sweet little girl of three to play with him."

"Yes," said Margery, nodding her head thoughtfully, "'at was it."

VI. A TWICE TOLD TALE

"Is that you, uncle?" said a voice from the nursery, as I hung my coat up in the hall. "I've only got my skin on, but you can come up."

However, she was sitting up in bed with her nightgown on when I found her.

"I was having my bath when you came," she explained. "Have you come all the way from London?"

"All the way."

"Then will you tell me a story?"

"I can't; I'm going to have my dinner. I only came up to say good night."

Margery leant forward and whispered coaxingly, "Will you just tell me about Beauty and 'e Beast?"

"But I've told you that such heaps of times. And it's much too long for to-night."

"Tell me *half* of it. As much as *that*." She held her hands about nine inches apart.

"That's too much."

"As much as *that*." The hands came a little nearer together.

"Oh! Well, I'll tell you up to where the Beast died."

"*Fought* he died," she corrected eagerly.

"Yes. Well——"

"How much will that be? As much as I said?"

I nodded. The preliminary business settled, she gave a little sigh of happiness, put her arms round her knees, and waited breathlessly for the story she had heard twenty times before.

"Once upon a time there was a man who had three daughters. And one day——"

"What was the man's name?"

"Margery," I said reproachfully, annoyed at the interruption, "you know I *never* tell you the man's name."

"Tell me now."

"Oswald," I said after a moment's thought.

"I told Daddy it was Thomas," said Margery casually.

"Well, as a matter of fact he had two names, Oswald *and* Thomas."

"Why did he have two names?"

"In case he lost one. Well, one day this man, who was very poor, heard that a lot of money was waiting for him in a ship which had come over the sea to a town some miles off. So he——"

"Was it waiting at Weymouf?"

"Somewhere like that."

"I spex it must have been Weymouf, because there's lots of sea there."

"Yes, I'm sure it was. Well, he thought he'd go to Weymouth and get the money."

"How much monies was it?"

"Oh, lots and lots."

"As much as five pennies?"

"Yes, about that. Well, he said good-bye to his daughters and asked them what they'd like him to bring back for a present. And the first asked for some lovely jewels and diamonds and——"

"Like Mummy's locket—is that jewels?"

"That sort of idea. Well, she wanted a lot of things like that. And the second wanted some beautiful clothes."

"What sort of clothes?"

"Oh, frocks and—well, frocks and all sorts of—er frocks."

"Did she want any lovely new stockings?"

"Yes, she wanted three pairs of those."

"And did she want any lovely——"

"Yes," I said hastily, "she wanted lots of those, too. Lots of *everything*."

Margery gave a little sob of happiness. "Go on telling me," she said under her breath.

"Well, the third daughter was called Beauty. And she thought to herself, 'Poor Father won't have any money left at all, if we all go on like this!' So she didn't ask for anything very expensive, like her selfish sisters, she only asked for a rose. A simple red rose."

Margery moved uneasily.

"I hope," she said wistfully, "this bit isn't going to be about—*you* know. It never did before."

"About what?"

"Good little girls and bad little girls, and fings like that."

"My darling, no, of course not. I told it wrong. Beauty asked for a rose because she loved roses so. And it was a very particular kind of red rose that she wanted—a sort that they simply *couldn't* get to grow in their own garden because of the soil."

"Go on telling me," said Margery, with a deep sigh of content.

"Well, he started off to Weymouth."

"What day did he start?"

"It was Monday. And when——"

"Oh, well, anyhow, I told Daddy it was Tuesday."

"Tuesday—now let me think. Yes, I believe you're right. Because on Monday he went to a meeting of the Vegetable Gardeners, and proposed the health of the Chairman. Yes, well he started off on Tuesday, and when he got there he found that there was no money for him at all!"

"I spex somebody had taken it," said Margery breathlessly.

"Well, it had all gone *somehow*."

"Prehaps somebody had swallowed it," said Margery, a little carried away by the subject, "by mistake."

"Anyhow, it was gone. And he had to come home again without any money. He hadn't gone far——"

"How far?" asked Margery. "As far as *that*?" and she measured nine inches in the air.

"About forty-four miles—when he came to a beautiful garden."

"Was it a really lovely big garden? Bigger than ours?"

"Oh, much bigger."

"Bigger than yours?"

"I haven't got a garden."

Margery looked at me wonderingly. She opened her mouth to speak, and then stopped and rested her head upon her hands and thought out this new situation. At last, her face flushed with happiness, she announced her decision.

"Go on telling me about Beauty and the Beast now," she said breathlessly, "and *then* tell me why you haven't got a garden."

My average time for Beauty and the Beast is ten minutes, and, if we stop at the place where the Beast thought he was dead, six minutes twenty-five seconds. But, with the aid of seemingly innocent questions, a determined character can make even the craftiest uncle spin the story out to half-an-hour.

"Next time," said Margery, when we had reached the appointed place and she was being tucked up in bed, "will you tell me *all* the story?"

Was there the shadow of a smile in her eyes? I don't know. But I'm sure it will be wisest next time to promise her the whole thing. We must make that point clear at the very start, and then we shall get along.

VII. THE LITERARY ART

Margery has a passion for writing just now. I can see nothing in it myself, but if people *will* write I suppose you can't stop them.

"Will you just lend me your pencil?" she asked.

"Remind me to give you a hundred pencils some time," I said as I took it out, "and then you'll always have one. You simply eat pencils."

"Oo, I gave it you back last time."

"Only just. You inveigle me down here——"

"What do I do?"

"I'm not going to say that again for anybody."

"Well, may I have the pencil?"

I gave her the pencil and a sheet of paper, and settled her in a chair.

"B-a-b-y," said Margery to herself, planning out her weekly article for the Reviews. "B-a-b-y, baby." She squared her elbows and began to write....

"There!" she said, after five minutes' composition.

The manuscript was brought over to the critic, and the author stood proudly by to point out subtleties that might have been overlooked at a first reading.

"B-a-b-y," explained the author. "Baby."

"Yes, that's very good; very neatly expressed. 'Baby'—I like that."

"Shall I write some more?" said Margery eagerly.

"Yes, do write some more. This is good, but it's not long enough."

The author retired again, and in five minutes produced this:

B A B Y

"That's 'baby,'" explained Margery.

"Yes, I like that baby better than the other one. It's more spread out. And it's bigger—it's one of the biggest babies I've seen."

"Shall I write some more?"

"Don't you write anything else ever?"

"I like writing 'baby,'" said Margery carelessly. "B-a-b-y."

"Yes, but you can't do much with just that one word. Suppose you wanted to write to a man at a shop—'Dear Sir, You never sent me my boots. Please send them at once as I want to go out this afternoon. I am yours faithfully, Margery'—it would be no good simply putting 'B-a-b-y,' because he wouldn't know what you meant."

"Well, what *would* it be good putting?"

"Ah, that's the whole art of writing—to know what it would be any good putting. You want to learn lots and lots of new words, so as to be ready. Now here's a jolly little one that you ought to meet." I took the pencil and wrote G O T. "Got. G-o-t, got."

Margery, her elbows on my knee and her chin resting on her hands, studied the position.

"Yes, that's old 'got,'" she said.

"He's always coming in. When you want to say, 'I've got a bad pain, so I can't accept your kind invitation'; or when you want to say, 'Excuse more, as I've got to go to bed now'; or quite simply, 'You've got my pencil.'"

"G-o-t, got," said Margery. "G-o-t, got. G-o-t, got."

"With appropriate action it makes a very nice recitation."

"Is that a 'g'?" said Margery, busy with the pencil, which she had snatched from me.

"The gentleman with the tail. You haven't made his tail quite long enough.... That's better."

Margery retired to her study charged with an entirely new inspiration, and wrote her second manifesto. It was this:

G O T

"Got," she pointed out.

I inspected it carefully. Coming fresh to the idea Margery had treated it more spontaneously than the other. But it was distinctly a "got." One of the gots.

"Have you any more words?" she asked, holding tight to the pencil.

"You've about exhausted me, Margery."

"What was that one you said just now? The one you said you wouldn't say again?"

"Oh, you mean 'inveigle'?" I said, pronouncing it differently this time.

"Yes; write that for me."

"It hardly ever comes in. Only when you are writing to your solicitor."

"What's 'solicitor'?"

"He's the gentleman who takes the money. He's *always* coming in."

"Then write 'solicitor.'"

I took the pencil (it was my turn for it) and wrote SOLICITOR. Then I read it out slowly to Margery, spelt it to her three times very carefully, and wrote SOLICITOR again. Then I said it thoughtfully to myself half-a-dozen times—"Solicitor." Then I looked at it wonderingly.

"I am not sure now," I said, "that there is such a word."

"Why?"

"I thought there was when I began, but now I don't think there can be. 'Solicitor'—it seems so silly."

"Let me write it," said Margery, eagerly taking the paper and pencil, "and see if it looks silly."

She retired, and—as well as she could for her excitement—copied the word down underneath. The combined effort then read as follows:

SOLICITOR
SOLICITOR
SOLCTOR

"Yes, you've done it a lot of good," I said. "You've taken some of the creases out. I like that much better."

"Do you think there is such a word now?"

"I'm beginning to feel more easy about it. I'm not certain, but I hope."

"So do I," said Margery. With the pencil in one hand and the various scraps of paper in the other, she climbed on to the writing desk and gave herself up to literature....

And it seems to me that she is well equipped for the task. For besides having my pencil still (of which I say nothing for the moment) she has now three separate themes upon which to ring the changes—a range wide enough for any writer. These are, "Baby got solicitor" (supposing that there is such a word), "Solicitor got baby," and "Got baby solicitor." Indeed, there are really four themes here, for the last one can have two interpretations. It might mean that you had obtained an ordinary solicitor for Baby or it might mean that you had got a specially small one for yourself. It lacks, therefore, the lucidity of the best authors, but in a woman writer this may be forgiven.

VIII. MY SECRETARY

When, five years ago, I used to write long letters to Margery, for some reason or other she never wrote back. To save her face I had to answer the letters myself—a tedious business. Still, I must admit that the warmth and geniality of the replies gave me a certain standing with my friends, who had not looked for me to be so popular. After some months, however, pride stepped in. One cannot pour out letter after letter to a lady without any acknowledgment save from oneself. And when even my own acknowledgments began to lose their first warmth—when, for instance, I answered four pages about my new pianola with the curt reminder that I was learning to walk and couldn't be bothered with music, why, then at last I saw that a correspondence so one-sided would have to come to an end. I wrote a farewell letter and replied to it with tears....

But, bless you, that was nearly five years ago. Each morning now, among the usual pile of notes on my plate from duchesses, publishers, moneylenders, actor-managers and what-not, I find, likely enough, an envelope in Margery's own handwriting.

Not only is my address printed upon it legibly, but there are also such extra directions to the postman as "England" and "Important" for its more speedy arrival. And inside—well, I give you the last but seven.

"MY DEAR UNCLE I thot you wher coming to see me to night but you didnt why didnt you baby has p t o hurt her knee isnt that a pity I have some new toys isnt that jolly we didnt have our five minutes so will you krite to me and tell me all about p t o your work from your loving little MARGIE."

I always think that footnotes to a letter are a mistake, but there are one or two things I should like to explain.

(a) Just as some journalists feel that without the word "economic" a leading article lacks tone, so Margery feels, and I agree with her, that a certain *cachet* is lent to a letter by a p. t. o. at the bottom of each page.

(b) There are lots of grown-up people who think that "write" is spelt "rite." Margery knows that this is not so. She knows that there is a silent letter in front of the "r," which doesn't do anything, but likes to be there. Obviously, if nobody is going to take any notice of this extra letter, it doesn't much matter what it is. Margery happened to want to make a "k" just then; at a pinch it could be as silent as a "w." You will please, therefore, regard the "k" in "Krite" as absolutely noiseless.

(c) Years ago I claimed the privilege to monopolise on the occasional evenings when I was there, Margery's last ten minutes before she goes back to some heaven of her own each night. This privilege was granted; it being felt, no doubt, that she owed me some compensation for my early secretarial work on her behalf. We used to spend the ten minutes in listening to my telling a fairy story, always the same one. One day the authorities stepped in and announced that in future the ten minutes would be reduced to five. The procedure seemed to me absolutely illegal (and I should like to bring an action against somebody) but it certainly did put the lid on my fairy story, of which I was getting more than a little tired.

"Tell me about Beauty and the Beast," said Margery as usual, that evening.

"There's not time," I said. "We've only five minutes to-night."

"Oh! Then tell me all the work you've done to-day."

(A little unkind, you'll agree, but you know what relations are.)

And so now I have to cram the record of my day's work into five breathless minutes. You will understand what bare justice I can do it in the time.

I am sorry that these footnotes have grown so big; let us leave them and return to the letter. There are many ways of answering such a letter. One might say, "MY DEAR MARGERY,—It was jolly to get a real letter from you at last——" but the "at last" would seem rather tactless considering what had passed years before. Or one might say, "MY DEAR MARGERY,—Thank you for your jolly letter. I am so sorry about baby's knee and so glad about your toys. Perhaps if you gave one of the toys to baby, then her knee——" But I feel sure that Margery would expect me to do better than that.

In the particular case of this last letter but seven I wrote:

"DEAREST MARGERY,—Thank you for your sweet letter. I had a very busy day at the office or I would have come to see you. P.T.O.

—I hope to be down next week and then I will tell you all about my work; but I have a lot more to do now, and so I must say good-bye. Your loving UNCLE."

There is perhaps nothing in that which demands an immediate answer, but with business-like promptitude Margery replied:

"MY DEAR UNCLE thank you for your letter I am glad you are coming next week baby is quite well now are you p t o coming on Thursday next week or not say yes if you are I am p t o sorry you are working so hard from your loving MARGIE."

I said "Yes," and that I was her loving uncle. It seemed to be then too late for a "P.T.O.," but I got one in and put on the back, "Love to Baby." The answer came by return of post:

"MY DEAR UNCLE thank you for your letter come erly on p t o Thursday come at half past nothing baby sends her love and so do p t o I my roking horse has a sirrup broken isnt that a pity say yes or no good-bye from your loving MARGIE."

Of course I thanked Baby for her love and gave my decision that it *was* a pity about the rocking-horse. I did it in large capitals, which (as I ought to have said before) is the means of communication between Margery and her friends. For some reason or other I find printing capitals to be more tiring than the ordinary method of writing.

"MY DEAR UNCLE," wrote Margery—

But we need not go into that. What I want to say is this: I love to get letters, particularly these, but I hate writing them, particularly in capitals. Years ago I used to answer Margery's letter for her. It is now her turn to answer mine for me.

IX. THE TRUTH ABOUT HOME RAILS

Imagine us, if you can, sitting one on each side of the fire, I with my feet on the mantelpiece, Margery curled up in the blue arm-chair, both of us intent on the morning paper. To me, by good chance, has fallen the sporting page; to Margery, the foreign, political and financial intelligence of the day.

"What," said Margery, "does it mean when it says——" she stopped and spelt it over to herself again.

I put down my piece of the paper and prepared to explain. The desire for knowledge in the young cannot be too strongly encouraged, and I have always flattered myself that I can explain in perfectly simple language anything which a child wants to know. For instance, I once told Margery what "Miniature Rifle Shooting" meant; it was a head-line which she had come across in her paper. The explanation took some time, owing to Margery's pre-conceived idea that a bird entered into it somewhere; several times, when I thought the lesson was over, she said, "Well, what about the bird?" But I think I made it plain to her in the end, though maybe she has forgotten about it now.

"What," said Margery, "does it mean when it says 'Home Rails Firm'?"

I took up my paper again. The Cambridge fifteen I was glad to see, were rapidly developing into a first-class team, and——

"'Home Rails Firm,'" repeated Margery, and looked up at me.

My mind worked rapidly, as it always does in a crisis.

"What did you say?" I asked in surprise.

"What does 'Home Rails Firm' mean?"

"Where does it say that?" I went on, still thinking at lightning speed.

"There. It said it yesterday too."

"Ah, yes." I made up my mind. "Well, that," I said—"I think that is something you must ask your father."

"I did ask him yesterday."

"Well, then——"

"He told me to ask Mummy."

Coward!

"You can be sure," I said firmly, "that what Mummy told you would be right," and I returned to my paper.

"Mummy told me to wait till *you* came."

Really, these parents! The way they shirk their responsibilities nowadays is disgusting.

"'Home Rails Firm.'" said Margery, and settled herself to listen.

It is good that children should be encouraged to take an interest in the affairs of the day, but I do think that a little girl might be taught by its father (or if more convenient, mother) which part of a newspaper to read. Had Margery asked me the difference between a bunker and a banker, had she demanded an explanation of "ultimatum" or "guillotine," I could have done something with it; but to let a child of six fill her head with ideas as to the firmness or otherwise of Home Rails is hardly nice. However, an explanation had to be given.

"Well, it's like this, Margery," I said at last. "Supposing—well—you see, supposing,—that is to say, if I——" and then I stopped. I had a sort of feeling—intuition, they call it—that I was beginning in the wrong way.

"Go on," said Margery.

"Perhaps, I had better put it this way. Supposing you were to—Well, we'd better begin further back than that. You know what—No, I don't suppose you do know that. Well, if I—that is to say, when a man—you know, it's rather difficult to explain this, Margery."

"Are you explaining it now?"

"I'm just going to begin."

"Thank you, uncle."

I lit my pipe slowly, while I considered again how best to approach the matter.

"'Home Rails Firm,'" said Margery. "Isn't it a *funny* thing to say?"

It was. It was a very silly thing to say. Whoever said it first might have known what it would lead to.

"Perhaps I can explain it best like this, Margery," I said, beginning on a new tack. "I suppose you know what 'firm' means?"

"What does it mean?"

"Ah, well, if you don't know that," I said, rather pleased, "perhaps I had better explain that first. 'Firm' means that—that is to say, you call a thing firm if it—well, if it doesn't—that is to say, a thing is firm if it can't move."

"Like a house."

"Well, something like that. This chair for instance," and I put my hand on her chair, "is firm because you can't shake it. You see, it's quite—Hallo, what's that?"

"Oh, you bad uncle, you've knocked the castor off again," cried Margery, greatly excited at the incident.

"This is too much," I said bitterly. "Even the furniture is against me."

"Go on explaining," said Margery, rocking herself in the now wobbly chair.

I decided to leave "firm." It is not an easy word to explain at the best of times, and when everything you touch goes and breaks itself it becomes perfectly impossible.

"Well, so much for that," I said. "And now we come to 'rails.' You know what rails are?"

"Like I've got in the nursery?"

This was splendid. I had forgotten these for the moment.

"Exactly. The rails your train goes on. Well, then, 'Home Rails' would be rails at home."

"Well, I've got them at home," said Margery in surprise. "I couldn't have them anywhere else."

"Quite so. Then 'Home Rails Firm' would mean that—er—home rails were—er—firm."

"But mine aren't, because they wobble. You know they do."

"Yes, but——"

"Well, why do they say 'Home Rails Firm' when they mean 'Home Rails Wobble'?"

"Ah, that's just it. The point is that when they say 'Home Rails Firm,' they don't mean that the rails themselves are firm. In fact they don't mean at all what you think they mean. They mean something quite different."

"What do they mean?"

"I am just going to explain," I said stiffly.

"Or perhaps I had better put it this way," I said ten minutes later. "Supposing—Oh, Margery, it is difficult to explain."

"I must know," said Margery.

"Why do you want to know so badly?"

"I want to know a million million times more than anything else in the whole world."

"Why?"

"So as I can tell Angela," said Margery.

I plunged into my explanation again. Angela is three, and I can quite see how important it is that she should be sound on the question.

LIFE'S LITTLE TRAGEDIES

X. A CROWN OF SORROWS

There is something on my mind, of which I must relieve myself. If I am ever to face the world again with a smile I must share my trouble with others. I cannot bear my burden alone.

Friends, I have lost my hat. Will the gentleman who took it by mistake, and forgot to leave his own in its place, kindly return my hat to me at once?

I am very miserable without my hat. It was one of those nice soft ones with a dent down the middle to collect the rain; one of those soft hats which wrap themselves so lovingly round the cranium that they ultimately absorb the personality of the wearer underneath, responding to his every emotion. When people said nice things about me my hat would swell in sympathy; when they said nasty things, or when I had had my hair cut, it would adapt itself automatically to my lesser requirements. In a word, it fitted—and that is more than can be said for your hard, unyielding bowler.

My hat and I dropped into a hall of music one night last week. I placed it under the seat, put a coat on it to keep it warm, and settled down to enjoy myself. My hat could see nothing, but it knew that it would hear all about the entertainment on the way home. When the last moving picture had moved away, my hat and I prepared to depart together. I drew out the coat and felt around for my—Where on earth....

I was calm at first.

"Excuse me," I said politely to the man next to me, "but have you got two hats?"

"Several," he replied, mistaking my meaning.

I dived under the seat again, and came up with some more dust.

"Some one," I said to the programme girl, "has taken my hat."

"Have you looked under the seat for it?" she asked.

It was such a sound suggestion that I went under the seat for the third time.

"It may have been kicked further along," suggested another attendant. She walked up and down the row looking for it; and, in case somebody had kicked it into the row above, walked up and down that one too; and, in case somebody had kicked it on to the other side of the house, many other girls spread themselves in pursuit; and soon we had the whole pack hunting for it.

Then the fireman came up, suspecting the worst. I told him it was even worse than that—my hat had been stolen.

He had a flash of inspiration.

"Are you sure you brought it with you?" he asked.

The programme girls seemed to think that it would solve the whole mystery if I hadn't brought it with me.

"Are you sure you are the fireman?" I said coldly.

He thought for a moment, and then unburdened himself of another idea.

"Perhaps it's just been kicked under the seat," he said.

I left him under the seat and went downstairs with a heavy heart. At the door I said to the hall porter, "Have you seen anybody going out with two hats by mistake?"

"What's the matter?" he said. "Lost your hat?"

"It has been stolen."

"Have you looked under the seats? It may have been kicked along a bit."

"Perhaps I'd better see the manager," I said. "Is it any good looking under the seats for *him*?"

"I expect it's just been kicked along a bit," the hall porter repeated confidently. "I'll come up with you and look for it."

"If there's any more talk about being kicked along a bit," I said bitterly, "somebody *will* be. I want the manager."

I was led to the manager's room, and there I explained the matter to him. He was very pleasant about it.

"I expect you haven't looked for it properly," he said, with a charming smile. "Just take this gentleman up," he added to the hall porter, "and find his hat for him. It has probably been kicked under one of the other seats."

We were smiled irresistibly out, and I was dragged up to the grand circle again. The seats by this time were laid out in white draperies; the house looked very desolate; I knew that my poor hat was dead.

With an air of cheery confidence the hall porter turned into the first row of seats....

"It may have been kicked on to the stage," I said, as he began to slow down. "It may have jumped into one of the boxes. It may have turned into a rabbit. You know, I expect you aren't looking for it properly."

The manager was extremely sympathetic when we came back to him. He said, "Oh, I'm sorry." Just like that—"Oh, I'm sorry."

"My hat," I said firmly, "has been stolen."

"I'm sorry," he repeated with a bored smile, and turned to look at himself in the glass.

Then I became angry with him and his attendants and his whole blessed theatre.

"My hat," I said bitingly, "has been stolen from me—while I slept."

You must have seen me wearing it in the dear old days. Greeny brown it was in colour; but it wasn't the colour that drew your eyes to it—no, nor yet the shape, nor the angle at which it sat. It was just the essential rightness of it. If you have ever seen a hat which you felt instinctively was a clever hat, an alive hat, a profound hat, then that was my hat—and that was myself underneath it.

XI. THE LUCKY MONTH

"Know thyself," said the old Greek motto. (In Greek—but this is an English book.) So I bought a little red volume called, tersely enough, *Were you born in January?* I was; and, reassured on this point, the author told me all about myself.

For the most part he told me nothing new. "You are," he said in effect, "good-tempered, courageous, ambitious, loyal, quick to resent wrong, an excellent *raconteur*, and a leader of men." True. "Generous to a fault"—(Yes, I was overdoing that rather)—"you have a ready sympathy with the distressed. People born in this month will always keep their promises." And so on. There was no doubt that the author had the idea all right. Even when he went on to warn me of my weaknesses he maintained the correct note. "People born in January," he said, "must be on their guard against working too strenuously. Their extraordinarily active brains——" Well, you see what he means. It *is* a fault perhaps, and I shall be more careful in future. Mind, I do not take offence with him for calling my attention to it. In fact, my only objection to the book is its surface application to *all* the people who were born in January. There should have been more distinction made between me and the rabble.

I have said that he told me little that was new. In one matter, however, he did open my eyes. He introduced me to an aspect of myself entirely unsuspected.

"They," he said—meaning me, "have unusual business capacity, and are destined to be leaders in great commercial enterprises."

One gets at times these flashes of self-revelation. In an instant I realised how wasted my life had been; in an instant I resolved that here and now I would put my great gifts to their proper uses. I would be a leader in an immense commercial enterprise.

One cannot start commercial enterprises without capital. The first thing was to determine the exact nature of my balance at the bank. This was a matter for the bank to arrange, and I drove there rapidly.

"Good morning," I said to the cashier, "I am in rather a hurry. May I have my pass-book?"

He assented and retired. After an interminable wait, during which many psychological moments for commercial enterprise must have lapsed, he returned.

"I think *you* have it," he said shortly.

"Thank you," I replied, and drove rapidly home again.

A lengthy search followed; but after an hour of it one of those white-hot flashes of thought, such as only occur to the natural business genius, seared my mind and sent me post-haste to the bank again.

"After all," I said to the cashier, "I only want to know my balance. What is it?"

He withdrew and gave himself up to calculation. I paced the floor impatiently. Opportunities were slipping by. At last he pushed a slip of paper across at me. My balance!

It was in four figures. Unfortunately two of them were shillings and pence. Still, there was a matter of fifty pounds odd as well, and fortunes have been built up on less.

Out in the street I had a moment's pause. Hitherto I had regarded my commercial enterprise in the bulk, as a finished monument of industry; the little niggling preliminary details had not come up for consideration. Just for a second I wondered how to begin.

Only for a second. An unsuspected talent which has long lain dormant needs, when waked, a second or so to turn round in. At the end of that time I had made up my mind. I knew exactly what I would do. I would ring up my solicitor.

"Hallo, is that you? Yes, this is me. What? Yes, awfully, thanks. How are you? Good. Look here, come and lunch with me. What? No, at once. Good-bye."

Business, particularly that sort of commercial enterprise to which I had now decided to lend my genius, can only be discussed properly over a cigar. During the meal itself my solicitor and I indulged in the ordinary small-talk of the pleasure-loving world.

"You're looking very fit," said my solicitor. "No, not fat, *fit*."

"You don't think I'm looking thin?" I asked anxiously. "People are warning me that I may be overdoing it rather. They tell me that I must be seriously on my guard against brain strain."

"I suppose they think you oughtn't to strain it too suddenly," said my solicitor. Though he is now a solicitor he was once just an ordinary boy like the rest of us, and it was in those days that he acquired the habit of being rude to me, a habit he has never quite forgotten.

"What is an onyx?" I said, changing the conversation.

"Why?" asked my solicitor, with his usual business acumen.

"Well, I was practically certain that I had seen one in the Zoo, in the reptile house, but I have just learnt that it is my lucky month stone. Naturally I want to get one."

The coffee came and we settled down to commerce.

"I was just going to ask you," said my solicitor—"have you any money lying idle at the bank? Because if so——"

"Whatever else it is doing, it isn't lying idle," I protested. "I was at the bank to-day, and there were men chivying it about with shovels all the time."

"Well, how much have you got?"

"About fifty pounds."

"It ought to be more than that."

"That's what I say, but you know what those banks are. Actual merit counts for nothing with them."

"Well, what did you want to do with it?"

"Exactly. That was why I rang you up. I—er——" This was really my moment, but somehow I was not quite ready to seize it. My vast commercial enterprise still lacked a few trifling details. "Er—I—well, it's like that."

"I might get you a few ground rents."

"Don't. I shouldn't know where to put them."

"But if you really have fifty pounds simply lying idle I wish you'd lend it to me for a bit. I'm confoundedly hard up."

("*Generous to a fault, you have a ready sympathy with the distressed.*" Dash it, what could I do?)

"Is it quite etiquette for clients to lend solicitors money?" I asked. "I thought it was always solicitors who had to lend it to clients. If I must, I'd rather lend it to you—I mean I'd dislike it less—as to the old friend of my childhood."

"Yes, that's how I wanted to pay it back."

"Bother. Then I'll send you a cheque to-night," I sighed.

And that's where we are at the moment. "*People born in this month always keep their promises.*" The money has got to go to-night. If I hadn't been born in January, I shouldn't be sending it; I certainly shouldn't have promised it; I shouldn't even have known that I had it. Sometimes I almost wish that I had been born in one of the decent months. March, say.

XII. THE RESCUE

William Bales—as nice a young man as ever wore a cummerbund on an esplanade—was in despair. For half-an-hour he and Miss Spratt had been sitting in silence on the pier, and it was still William's turn to say something. Miss Spratt's last remark had been, "Oh, Mr. Bales, you do say things!" and William felt that his next observation must at all costs live up to the standard set for it. Three or four times he had opened his mouth to speak, and then on second thoughts had rejected the intended utterance as unworthy. At the end of half-an-hour his mind was still working fruitlessly. He knew that the longer he waited the more brilliant he would have to be, and he told himself that even Bernard Shaw or one of those clever writing fellows would have been hard put to it now.

William was at odds with the world. He was a romantic young man who had once been told that he nearly looked like Lewis Waller when he frowned, and he had resolved that his holiday this year should be a very dashing affair indeed. He had chosen the sea in the hopes that some old gentleman would fall off the pier and let himself be saved by—and, later on, photographed with—William Bales, who in a subsequent interview would modestly refuse to take any credit for the gallant rescue. As his holiday had progressed he had felt the need for some such old gentleman more and more; for only thus, he realised, could he capture the heart of the wayward Miss Spratt. But so far it had been a dull season; in a whole fortnight nobody had gone out of his way to oblige William, and to-morrow he must return to the City as unknown and as unloved as when he left it.

"Got to go back to-morrow," he said at last. As an impromptu it would have served, but as the result of half-an-hour's earnest thought he felt that it did not do him justice.

"So you said before," remarked Miss Spratt.

"Well, it's still true."

"Talking about it won't help it," said Miss Spratt.

William sighed and looked round the pier. There was an old gentleman fishing at the end of it, his back turned invitingly to William. In half-an-hour he had caught one small fish (which he had had to return as under the age limit) and a bunch of seaweed. William felt that here was a wasted life; a life, however, which a sudden kick and a heroic rescue by W. Bales might yet do something to justify. At the Paddington Baths, a month ago, he had won a plate-diving competition; and, though there is a difference between diving for plates and diving for old gentlemen, he was prepared to waive it. One kick and then ... Fame! And, not only Fame, but the admiration of Angelina Spratt.

It was perhaps as well for the old gentleman—who was really quite worthy, and an hour later caught a full-sized whiting—that Miss Spratt spoke at this moment.

"Well, you're good company, I must say," she observed to William.

"It's so hot," said William.

"You can't say I asked to come here."

"Let's go on the beach," said William desperately. "We can find a shady cave or something." Fate was against him; there was to be no rescue that day.

"I'm sure I'm agreeable," said Miss Spratt.

They walked in silence along the beach, and, rounding a corner of the cliffs, they came presently to a cave. In earlier days W. Bales could have done desperate deeds against smugglers there, with Miss Spratt looking on. Alas for this unromantic age! It was now a place for picnics, and a crumpled sheet of newspaper on the sand showed that there had been one there that very afternoon.

They sat in a corner of the cave, out of the sun, out of sight of the sea, and William prepared to renew his efforts as a conversationalist. In the hope of collecting a few ideas as to what the London clubs were talking about he picked up the discarded newspaper, and saw with disgust that it was the local *Herald*. But just as he threw it down, a line in it caught his eye and remained in his mind——

"*High tide to-day—3.30.*"

William's heart leapt. He looked at his watch; it was 2.30. In one hour the waves would be dashing remorselessly into the cave, would be leaping up the cliff, what time he and Miss Spratt——

Suppose they were caught by the tide....

Meanwhile the lady, despairing of entertainment, had removed her hat.

"Really," she said, "I'm that sleepy—I suppose the tide's safe, Mr. Bales?"

It was William's chance.

"Quite, quite safe," he said earnestly. "It's going down hard."

"Well, then, I almost think——" She closed her eyes. "Wake me up when you've thought of something really funny, Mr. Bales."

William was left alone with Romance.

He went out of the cave and looked round. The sea was still some way out, but it came up quickly on this coast. In an hour ... in an hour....

He scanned the cliffs, and saw the ledge whither he would drag her. She would cling to him crying, calling him her rescuer....

What should he do then? Should he leave her and swim for help? Or should he scale the mighty cliff?

He returned to the cave and, gazing romantically at the sleeping Miss Spratt, conjured up the scene. It would go like this, he thought.

Miss Spratt (wakened by the spray dashing over her face). Oh, Mr. Bales! We're cut off by the tide! Save me!

W. Bales (lightly). Tut-tut, there's no danger. It's nothing. (*Aside*) Great Heavens! Death stares us in the face!

Miss Spratt (throwing her arms around his neck). William, save me; I cannot swim!

W. Bales (with Waller face). Trust me, Angelina. I will fight my way round yon point and obtain help. (*Aside*) An Englishman can only die once.

Miss Spratt. Don't leave me!

W. Bales. Fear not, sweetheart. See, there is a ledge where you will be beyond the reach of the hungry tide. I will carry you thither in my arms and will then——

At this point in his day-dream William took another look at the sleeping Miss Spratt, felt his biceps doubtfully, and went on—

W. Bales. I will assist you to climb thither, and will then swim for help.

Miss Spratt. My hero!

Again and again William reviewed the scene to himself. It was perfect. His photograph would be in the papers; Miss Spratt would worship him; he would be a hero in his City office. The actual danger was slight, for at the worst she could shelter in the far end of the cave; but he would not let her know this. He would do the thing heroically—drag her to the ledge on the cliff, and then swim round the point to obtain help.

The thought struck him that he could conduct the scene better in his shirt sleeves. He removed his coat, and then went out of the cave to reconnoitre the ledge.

Miss Spratt awoke with a start and looked at her watch. It was 4.15. The cave was empty save for a crumpled page of newspaper. She glanced at this idly and saw that it was the local *Herald* ... eight days old.

Far away on the horizon William Bales was throwing stones bitterly at the still retreating sea.

XIII. THE PORTUGUESE CIGAR

Everything promised well for my week-end with Charles. The weather was warm and sunny, I was bringing my golf clubs down with me, and I had just discovered (and meant to put into practice) an entirely new stance which made it impossible to miss the object ball. It was this that I was explaining to Charles and his wife at dinner on Friday, when the interruption occurred.

"By the way," said Charles, as I took out a cigarette, "I've got a cigar for you. Don't smoke that thing."

"You haven't let him go in for cigars?" I said reproachfully to Mrs. Charles. I can be very firm about other people's extravagances.

"This is one I picked up in Portugal," explained Charles. "You can get them absurdly cheap out there. Let's see, dear; where did I put it?"

"I saw it on your dressing-table last week," said his wife, getting up to leave us. He followed her out and went in search of it, while I waited with an interest which I made no effort to conceal. I had never heard before of a man going all the way to Portugal to buy one cigar for a friend.

"Here it is," said Charles, coming in again. He put down in front of me an ash-tray, the matches and a—and a—well, a cigar. I examined it slowly. Half of it looked very tired.

"Well," said Charles, "what do you think of it?"

"When you say you—er—*picked it up* in Portugal," I began carefully, "I suppose you don't mean——" I stopped and tried to bite the end off.

"Have a knife," said Charles.

I had another bite, and then I decided to be frank.

"*Why* did you pick it up?" I asked.

"The fact was," said Charles, "I found myself one day in Lisbon without my pipe, and so I bought that thing; I never smoke them in the ordinary way."

"Did you smoke this?" I asked. It was obvious that *something* had happened to it.

"No, you see, I found some cigarettes at the last moment, and so, knowing that you liked cigars, I thought I'd bring it home for you."

"It's very nice of you, Charles. Of course I can see that it has travelled. Well, we must do what we can with it."

I took the knife and started chipping away at the mahogany end. The other end—the brown-paper end, which had come ungummed—I intended to reserve for the match. When everything was ready I applied a light, leant back in my chair, and pulled.

"That's all right, isn't it?" said Charles. "You'd be surprised if I told you what I paid for it."

"No, no, you mustn't think that," I protested. "Probably things are dearer in Portugal." I put it down by my plate for a moment's rest. "All I've got against it at present is that its pores don't act as freely as they should."

"I've got a cigar-cutter somewhere, if——"

"No, don't bother, I think I can do it with the nut-crackers. There's no doubt it was a good cigar once, but it hasn't wintered well."

I squeezed it as hard as I could, lit it again, pressed my feet against the table and pulled.

"Now it's going," said Charles.

"I'm afraid it keeps very reticent at my end. The follow-through is poor. Is your end alight still?"

"Burning beautifully."

"It's a pity that I should be missing all that. How would it be if we were to make a knitting-needle red-hot and bore a tunnel from this end? We might establish a draught that way. Only there's always the danger, of course, of coming out at the side."

I took the cigar up and put it to my ear.

"I can't hear anything wrong," I said. "I expect what it really wants is massage."

Charles filled his pipe again and got up. "Let's go for a stroll," he said. "It's a beautiful night. Bring your cigar with you."

"It may prefer the open air," I said. "There's always that. You know we mustn't lose sight of the fact that the Portuguese climate is different from ours. The thing's pores may have acted more readily in the South. On the other hand, the unfastened end may have been more adhesive. I gather that though you have never actually met anybody who has smoked a cigar like this, yet you understand that the experiment is a practicable one. As far as you know this had no brothers. No, no, Charles, I'm going on with it, but I should like to know all that you can tell me of its parentage. It had a Portuguese father and an American mother, I should say, and there has been a good deal of trouble in the family. One moment"—and as we went outside I stopped and cracked it in the door.

It was an inspiration. At the very next application of the match I found that I had established a connection with the lighted end. Not a long and steady connection, but one that came in gusts. After two gusts I decided that it was perhaps safer to blow from my end, and for a little while we had in this way as much smoke around us as the most fastidious cigar-smoker could want. Then I accidentally dropped it; something in the middle of it shifted, I suppose—and for the rest of my stay behind it only one end was at work.

"Well," said Charles, when we were back in the smoking-room and I was giving the cigar a short breather, "it's not a bad one, is it?"

"I have enjoyed it," I said truthfully, for I like trying to get the mastery over a thing that defies me.

"You'll never guess what it cost," he chuckled.

"Tell me," I said. "I daren't guess."

"Well, in English money it works out at exactly three farthings."

I looked at him for a long time and then shook my head sadly.

"Charles, old friend," I said, "you've been done."

XIV. A COLD WORLD

Herbert is a man who knows all about railway tickets, and packing, and being in time for trains, and things like that. But I fancy I have taught him a lesson at last. He won't talk quite so much about tickets in future.

I was just thinking about getting up when he came into my room. He looked at me in horror.

"My dear fellow!" he said. "And you haven't even packed! You'll be late. Here, get up, and I'll pack for you while you dress."

"Do," I said briefly.

"First of all, what clothes are you going to travel in?"

There was no help for it. I sat up in bed and directed operations.

"Right," said Herbert. "Now what about your return ticket? You mustn't forget that."

"You remind me of a little story," I said. "I'll tell it you while you pack—that will be nice for you. Once upon a time I lost my return ticket, and I had to pay two pounds for another. And a month afterwards I met a man—a man like you who knows all about tickets—and he said, 'You could have got the money back if you had applied at once.' So I said, 'Give me a cigarette now, and I'll transfer all my rights in the business to you.' And he gave me a cigarette; but unfortunately——"

"It was too late?"

"No. Unfortunately it wasn't. He got the two pounds. The most expensive cigarette I've ever smoked."

"Well, that just shows you," said Herbert. "Here's your ticket. Put it in your waistcoat pocket now."

"But I haven't got a waistcoat on, silly."

"Which one are you going to put on?"

"I don't know yet. This is a matter which requires thought. Give me time, give me air."

"Well, I shall put the ticket here on the dressing-table, and then you can't miss it." He looked at his watch. "And the trap starts in half an hour."

"Help!" I cried, and I leapt out of bed.

Half an hour later I was saying good-bye to Herbert.

"I've had an awfully jolly time," I said, "and I'll come again."

"You've got the ticket all right?"

"Rather!" and I drove away amidst cheers. Cheers of sorrow.

It was half-an-hour's drive to the station. For the first five minutes I thought how sickening it was to be leaving the country; then I had a slight shock; and for the next twenty-five minutes I tried to remember how much a third single to the nearest part of London cost. Because I had left my ticket on the dressing-table after all.

I gave my luggage to a porter and went off to the station-master.

"I wonder if you can help me," I said. "I've left my ticket on the dress—— Well, we needn't worry about that, I've left it at home."

He didn't seem intensely excited.

"What did you think of doing?" he asked.

"I had rather hoped that *you* would do something."

"You can buy another ticket, and get the money back afterwards."

"Yes, yes; but can I? I've only got about one pound six."

"The fare to London is one pound five and tenpence ha'penny."

"Ah; well, that leaves a penny ha'penny to be divided between the porter this end, lunch, tea, the porter the other end, and the cab. I don't believe it's enough. Even if I gave it all to the porter here, think how reproachfully he would look at you ever afterwards. It would haunt you."

The station-master was evidently moved. He thought for a moment, and then asked if I knew anybody who would vouch for me. I mentioned Herbert confidently. He had never even heard of Herbert.

"I've got a tie-pin," I said (station-masters have a weakness for tie-pins), "and a watch and a cigarette case. I shall be happy to lend you any of those."

The idea didn't appeal to him.

"The best thing you can do," he said, "is to take a ticket to the next station and talk to them there. This is only a branch line, and I have no power to give you a pass."

So that was what I had to do. I began to see myself taking a ticket at every stop and appealing to the station-master at the next. Well, the money would last longer that way, but unless I could overcome quickly the distrust which I seemed to inspire in station-masters there would not be much left for lunch. I gave the porter all I could afford—a ha'penny, mentioned apologetically that I was coming back, and stepped into the train.

At the junction I jumped out quickly and dived into the sacred office.

"I've left my ticket on the dressing—that is to say, I forgot—— Well, anyhow, I haven't got it," I began, and we plunged into explanations once more. This station-master was even more unemotional than the last. He asked me if I knew anybody who could vouch for me. I mentioned Herbert diffidently. He had never even heard of Herbert. I showed him my gold watch, my silver cigarette case, and my emerald and diamond tie-pin—that was the sort of man I was.

"The best thing you can do," he said, walking with me to the door, "is to take a ticket to Plymouth, and speak to the station-master there——"

"This is a most interesting game," I said bitterly. "What is 'home'? When you speak to the station-master at London, I suppose? I've a good mind to say 'snap'!"

Extremely annoyed I strode out, and bumped into—you'll never guess—Herbert!

"Ah, here you are," he panted; "I rode after you—the train was just going—jumped into it—been looking all over the station for you."

"It's awfully nice of you, Herbert. Didn't I say good-bye?"

"Your ticket." He produced it. "Left it on the dressing-table." He took a deep breath. "I told you you would."

"Bless you," I said, as I got happily into my train. "You've saved my life. I've had an awful time. I say, do you know, I've met two station-masters already this morning who've never even heard of you. You must enquire into it."

At that moment a porter came up.

"Did you give up your ticket, Sir?" he asked Herbert.

"I hadn't time to get one," said Herbert, quite at his ease. "I'll pay now," and he began to feel in his pockets.... The train moved out of the station.

A look of horror came over Herbert's face. I knew what it meant. He hadn't any money on him. "Hi!" he shouted to me, and then we swung round a bend out of sight....

Well, well, he'll have to get home somehow. His watch is only nickel and his cigarette case leather, but luckily that sort of thing doesn't weigh much with station-masters. What they want is a well-known name as a reference. Herbert is better off than I was: he can give them *my* name. It will be idle for them to pretend that they have never heard of *me*.

XV. A BREATH OF LIFE

This is the story of a comedy which nearly became a tragedy. In its way it is rather a pathetic story.

The comedy was called "The Wooing of Winifred." It was written by an author whose name I forget; produced by the well-known and (as his press agent has often told us) popular actor-manager, Mr. Levinski; and played by (among others) that very charming young man, Prosper Vane—known locally as Alfred Briggs until he took to the stage. Prosper played the young hero, *Dick Seaton*, who was actually wooing *Winifred*. Mr. Levinski himself took the part of a middle-aged man of the world with a slight embonpoint; down in the programme as *Sir Geoffrey Throssell*, but fortunately still Mr. Levinski. His opening words, as he came on, were, "Ah, Dick, I have a note for you somewhere," which gave the audience an interval in which to welcome him, while he felt in all his pockets for the letter. One can bow quite easily while feeling in one's pockets, and it is much more natural than stopping in the middle of an important speech in order to acknowledge any cheers. The realisation of this, by a dramatist, is what is called "stagecraft." In this case the audience could tell at once that the "technique" of the author (whose name unfortunately I forget) was going to be all right.

But perhaps I had better describe the whole play as shortly as possible. The theme—as one guessed from the title, even before the curtain rose—was the wooing of *Winifred*. In the First Act Dick proposed to *Winifred* and was refused by her, not from lack of love, but for fear lest she might spoil his career, he being one of those big-hearted men with a hip-pocket to whom the open spaces of the world call loudly. Whereupon Mr. Levinski took *Winifred* on one side and told the audience how, when he had been a young man, some good woman had refused him for a similar reason and had been miserable ever since. Accordingly in the Second Act *Winifred* withdrew her refusal and offered to marry *Dick*, who declined to take advantage of her offer for fear that she was willing to marry him from pity rather than from love; whereupon Mr. Levinski took *Dick* on one side and told the audience how, when *he* had been a young man, he had refused to marry some good woman (a different one) for a similar reason, and had been broken-hearted ever afterwards. In the Third Act it really seemed as though they were coming together at last; for at the beginning of it Mr. Levinski took them both aside and told the audience a parable about a butterfly and a snap-dragon, which was both pretty and helpful, and caused several middle-aged ladies in the first and second rows of the upper circle to say, "What a nice man Mr. Levinski must be at home, dear!"—the purport of the allegory being to show that both *Dick* and *Winifred* were being very silly, as indeed by this time everybody but the author was aware. Unfortunately at that moment a footman entered with a telegram for *Miss Winifred*, which announced that she had been left fifty thousand pounds by a dead uncle in Australia; and although Mr. Levinski seized this fresh opportunity to tell the audience how in similar circumstances Pride, to his lasting remorse, had kept him and some good woman (a third one) apart, nevertheless *Dick* held back once more, for fear lest he should be thought to be marrying her for her money. The curtain comes down as he says, "Good-bye.... Good-ber-eye." But there is a Fourth Act, and in the Fourth Act Mr. Levinski has a splendid time. He tells the audience two parables—one about a dahlia and a sheep, which I couldn't quite follow—and three reminiscences of life in India; he brings together finally and for ever these hesitating lovers; and, best of all, he has a magnificent love-scene of his own with a pretty widow, in which we see, for the first time in the play, how love should really be made—not boy-and-girl pretty-pretty love, but the deep emotion felt (and with occasional lapses of memory explained) by a middle-aged man with a slight embonpoint who has knocked about the world a bit and knows life. Mr. Levinski, I need hardly say, was at his best in this Act.

I met Prosper Vane at the club some ten days before the first night, and asked him how rehearsals were going.

"Oh, all right," he said. "But it's a rotten play. I've got such a dashed silly part."

"From what you told me," I said, "it sounded rather good."

"It's so dashed unnatural. For three whole Acts this girl and I are in love with each other, and we know we're in love with each other, and yet we simply fool about. She's a dashed pretty girl too, my boy. In real life I'd jolly soon——"

"My dear Alfred," I protested, "you're not going to fall in love with the girl you have to fall in love with on the stage? I thought actors never did that."

"They do sometimes; it's a dashed good advertisement. Anyway, it's a silly part, and I'm fed up with it."

"Yes, but do be reasonable. If *Dick* got engaged at once to *Winifred* what would happen to Levinski? He'd have nothing to do."

Prosper Vane grunted. As he seemed disinclined for further conversation, I left him.

The opening night came, and the usual distinguished and fashionable audience (including myself) such as habitually attends Mr. Levinski's first nights, settled down to enjoy itself. Two Acts went well. At the end of each Mr. Levinski came before the curtain and bowed to us, and we had the honour of clapping him loud and long. Then the Third Act began....

Now this is how the Third Act ends:

Exit Sir Geoffrey.

Winifred (breaking the silence). Dick, you heard what he said. Don't let this silly money come between us. I have told you I love you, dear. Won't you—won't you speak to me?

Dick. Winifred, I—— *(He gets up and walks round the room, his brow knotted, his right fist occasionally striking his left palm. Finally, he comes to a stand in front of her.)* Winifred, I—— *(He raises his arms slowly at right angles to his body and lets them fall heavily down again.)* I can't. *(In a low hoarse voice)* I—can't! *(He stands for a moment with bent head; then with a jerk he pulls himself together.)* Good-bye! *(His hands go out to her, but he draws them back as if frightened to touch her. Nobly.)* Good-ber-eye.

He squares his shoulders and stands looking at the audience with his chin in the air; then with a shrug of utter despair, which would bring tears into the eyes of any young thing in the pit, he turns and with bent head walks slowly out.

CURTAIN.

That is how the Third Act ends. I went to the dress rehearsal, and so I know.

How the accident happened I do not know. I suppose Prosper was nervous. I am sure he was very much in love. Anyhow, this is how, on that famous first night, the Third Act ended:

Exit Sir Geoffrey.

Winifred (breaking the silence). Dick, you heard what he said. Don't let this silly money come between us. I have told you I love you, dear. Won't you—won't you speak to me?

Dick (jumping up). Winifred I—— *(with a great gulp)* I LOVE YOU!!!

Whereupon he picked her up in his arms and carried her triumphantly off the stage ... and after a little natural hesitation the curtain came down.

Behind the scenes all was consternation. Mr. Levinski (absolutely furious) had a hasty consultation with the author (also furious), in the course of which they both saw that the Fourth Act as written was now an impossibility. Poor Prosper, who had almost immediately recovered his sanity, tremblingly suggested that Mr. Levinski should announce that, owing to the sudden illness of Mr. Vane the Fourth Act could not be given. Mr. Levinski was kind enough to consider this suggestion not entirely stupid; his own idea having been (very regretfully) to leave out the two parables and three reminiscences from India, and concentrate on the love-scene with the widow.

"Yes, yes," he said. "Your plan is better. I will say you are ill. It is true; you are mad. To-morrow we will play it as it was written."

"You can't," said the author gloomily. "The critics won't come till the Fourth Act and they'll assume that the Third Act ended as it did to-night. The Fourth Act will seem all nonsense to them."

"True. And I was so good, so much myself in that Act." He turned to Prosper. "You—fool!"

"Or there's another way," began the author. "We might——"

And then a gentleman in the gallery settled it from the front of the curtain. There was nothing in the programme to show that the play was in four Acts. "The Time is the present-day and the Scene is in Sir Geoffrey Throssell's town-house," was all it said. And the gentleman in the gallery, thinking it was all over, and being pleased with the play and particularly with the realism of the last moment of it, shouted, "Author." And suddenly everybody else cried, "Author! Author." The Play was ended.

I said that this was the story of a comedy which nearly became a tragedy. But it turned out to be no tragedy at all. In the three Acts to which Prosper Vane had condemned it the play appealed to both critics and public, for the Fourth Act (as he recognised so clearly) was unnecessary, and would have spoilt the balance of it entirely. Best of all, the shortening of the play demanded that some entertainment should be provided in front of it, and this enabled Mr. Levinski to introduce to the public Professor Wollabollacolla and Princess Collabollawolla, the famous exponents of the Bongo-Bongo, that fascinating Central African war dance, which was soon to be the rage of society. But though, as a result, the takings of the Box Office surpassed all Mr. Levinski's previous records, our friend Prosper Vane received no practical acknowledgment of his services.

He had to be content with the hand and heart of the lady who played *Winifred*, and the fact that Mr. Levinski was good enough to attend the wedding. There was, in fact, a photograph in all the papers of Mr. Levinski doing it.

XVI. THE DOCTOR

"May I look at my watch?" I asked my partner, breaking a silence which had lasted from the beginning of the waltz.

"Oh, *have* you got a watch?" she drawled. "How exciting!"

"I wasn't going to show it to you," I said. "But I always think it looks so bad for a man to remove his arm from a lady's waist in order to look at his watch—I mean without some sort of apology or explanation. As though he were wondering if he could possibly stick another five minutes of it."

"Let me know when the apology is beginning," said Miss White. Perhaps, after all, her name wasn't White, but, anyhow, she was dressed in White, and it's her own fault if wrong impressions arise.

"It begins at once. I've got to catch a train home. There's one at 12.45, I believe. If I started now I could just miss it."

"You don't live in these Northern Heights, then?"

"No. Do you?"

"Yes."

I looked at my watch again.

"I should love to discuss with you the relative advantages of London and Greater London," I said; "the flats and cats of one and the big gardens of the other. But just at the moment the only thing I can think of is whether I shall like the walk home. Are there any dangerous passes to cross?"

"It's a nice wet night for a walk," said Miss White reflectively.

"If only I had brought my bicycle."

"A watch *and* a bicycle! You *are* lucky!"

"Look here, it may be a joke to you, but I don't fancy myself coming down the mountains at night."

"The last train goes at one o'clock, if that's any good to you."

"All the good in the world," I said joyfully. "Then I needn't walk." I looked at my watch. "That gives us five minutes more. I could almost tell you all about myself in that time."

"It generally takes longer than that," said Miss White. "At least it seems to." She sighed and added, "My partners have been very autobiographical to-night."

I looked at her severely.

"I'm afraid you're a Suffragette," I said.

As soon as the next dance began I hurried off to find my hostess. I had just caught sight of her when——

"Our dance, isn't it?" said a voice.

I turned and recognised a girl in blue.

"Ah," I said, coldly cheerful, "I was just looking for you. Come along."

We broke into a gay and happy step, suggestive of twin hearts utterly free from care.

"Why do you look so thoughtful?" asked the girl in blue after ten minutes of it.

"I've just heard some good news," I said.

"Oh, do tell me!"

"I don't know if it would really interest you."

"I'm sure it would."

"Well, several miles from here there may be a tram, if one can find it, which goes nobody quite knows where up till one-thirty in the morning probably. It is now," I added, looking at my watch (I was getting quite good at this), "just on one o'clock and raining hard. All is well."

The dance over, I searched in vain for my hostess. Every minute I took out my watch and seemed to feel that another tram was just starting off to some unknown destination. At last I could bear it no longer and, deciding to write a letter of explanation on the morrow, I dashed off.

My instructions from Miss White with regard to the habitat of trams (thrown in by her at the last moment in case the train failed me) were vague. Five minutes' walk convinced me that I had completely lost any good that they might ever have been to me. Instinct and common sense were the only guides left. I must settle down to some heavy detective work.

The steady rain had washed out any footprints that might have been of assistance, and I was unable to follow up the slot of a tram conductor of which I had discovered traces in Two-hundred-and-fifty-first Street. In Three-thousand-eight-hundred-and-ninety-seventh Street I lay with my ear to the ground and listened intently, for I seemed to hear the ting-ting of the electric car, but nothing came of it; and in Four-millionth Street I made a new resolution. I decided to give up looking for trams and to search instead for London—the London that I knew.

I felt pretty certain that I was still in one of the Home Counties, and I did not seem to remember having crossed the Thames, so that if only I could find a star which pointed to the south I was in a fair way to get home. I set out to look for a star; with the natural result that, having abandoned all hope of finding a man, I immediately ran into him.

"Now then," he said good-naturedly.

"Could you tell me the way to"—I tried to think of some place near my London—"to Westminster Abbey?"

He looked at me in astonishment. His feeling seemed to be that I was too late for the Coronation and too early for the morning service.

"Or—or anywhere," I said hurriedly. "Trams, for instance."

He pointed nervously to the right and disappeared.

Imagine my joy; there were tramlines, and better still, a tram approaching. I tumbled in, gave the conductor a penny, and got a workman's ticket in exchange. Ten minutes later we reached the terminus.

I had wondered where we should arrive, but didn't much mind so long as I was again within reach of a cab. However, as soon as I stepped out of the tram, I knew at once where I was.

"Tell me," I said to the conductor, "do you now go back again?"

"In ten minutes. There's a tram from here every half-hour."

"When is the last?"

"There's no last. Backwards and forwards all night."

I should have liked to stop and sympathise, but it was getting late. I walked a hundred yards up the hill and turned to the right.... As I entered the gates I could hear the sound of music.

"Isn't this our dance?" I said to Miss White, who was taking a breather at the hall door. "One moment," I added and I got out of my coat and umbrella.

"Is it? I thought you'd gone."

"Oh, no, I decided to stay, after all. I found out that the trams go all night."

We walked in together.

"I won't be more autobiographical than I can help," I said, "but I must say it's hard life, a doctor's. One is called away in the middle of a dance to a difficult case of—of mumps or something, and—well, there you are. A delightful evening spoilt. If one is lucky one may get back in time for a waltz or two at the end.

"Indeed," I said, as we began to dance, "at one time to-night I quite thought I wasn't going to get back here at all."

XVII. THE FINANCIER

This is how I became a West African mining magnate with a stake in the Empire.

During February I grew suddenly tired of waiting for the summer to begin. London in the summer is a pleasant place, and chiefly so because you can keep on buying evening papers to read the cricket news. In February life has no such excitements to offer. So I wrote to my solicitor about it.

"I want you," I wrote, "to buy me fifty rubber shares, so that I can watch them go up and down." And I added, "Brokerage one-eighth," to show that I knew what I was talking about.

He replied tersely as follows:

"Don't be a fool. If you have any money to invest I can get you a safe mortgage at five per cent. Let me know."

It's a funny thing how the minds of solicitors run upon mortgages. If they would only stop to think for a moment they would see that you couldn't possibly watch a safe mortgage go up and down. I left my solicitor alone and consulted Henry on the subject. In the intervals between golf and golf Henry dabbles in finance.

"You don't want anything gilt-edged, I gather," he said. It's wonderful how they talk.

"I want it to go up and down," I explained patiently, and I indicated the required movement with my umbrella.

"What about a little flutter in oil?" he went on, just like a financier in a novel.

"I'll have a little flutter in raspberry jam if you like. Anything as long as I can rush every night for the last edition of the evening papers and say now and then, 'Good heavens, I'm ruined!'"

"Then you'd better try a gold mine," said Henry bitterly, in the voice of one who has tried. "Take your choice," and he threw the paper over to me.

"I don't want a whole mine—only a vein or two. Yes, this is very interesting," I went on, as I got among the West Africans. "The scoring seems to be pretty low; I suppose it must have been a wet wicket. 'H.E. Reef, 1¾, 2'—he did a little better in the second innings. '½, Boffin River, 5/16, 7/16,—they followed on, you see, but they saved the innings defeat. By the way, which figure do I really keep my eye on when I want to watch them go up and down?"

"Both. One eye on each. And don't talk about Boffin River to *me*."

"Is it like that, Henry? I am sorry. I suppose it's too late now to offer you a safe mortgage at five per cent.? I know a man who has some. Well, perhaps you're right."

On the next day I became a magnate. The Jaguar Mine was the one I fixed upon—for two reasons. First, the figure immediately after it was 1, which struck me as a good point from which to watch it go up and down. Secondly, I met a man at lunch who knew somebody who had actually seen the Jaguar Mine.

"He says that there's no doubt about there being lots there."

"Lots of what? Jaguars or gold?"

"Ah, he didn't say. Perhaps he meant Jaguars."

Anyhow, it was an even chance, and I decided to risk it. In a week's time I was the owner of what we call in the City a "block" of Jaguars—bought from one Herbert Bellingham, who, I suppose, had been got at by his solicitor and compelled to return to something safe. I was a West African magnate.

My first two months as a magnate were a great success. With my heart in my mouth I would tear open the financial editions of the evening papers, to find one day that Jaguars had soared like a rocket to 1-1/16, the next that they had dropped like a stone to 1-1/32. There was one terrible afternoon when for some reason which will never be properly explained we sank to 15/16. I think the European situation had something to do with it, though this naturally is not admitted. Lord Rothschild, I fancy, suddenly threw all his Jaguars on the market; he sold and sold and sold, and only held his hand when, in desperation, the Tsar granted the concession for his new Southend to Siberia railway. Something like that. But he never recked how the private investor would suffer; and there was I, sitting at home and sending out madly for all the papers, until my rooms were littered with copies of *The Times*, *The Financial News*, *Answers*, *The Feathered World* and *Home Chat*. Next day we were up to 31/32, and I breathed again.

But I had other pleasures than these. Previously I had regarded the City with awe, but now I felt a glow of possession come over me whenever I approached it. Often in those first two months I used to lean against the Mansion House in a familiar sort of way; once I struck a match against the Royal Exchange. And what an impression of financial acumen I could make in a drawing-room by a careless reference to my "block of Jaguars!" Even those who misunderstood me and thought I spoke of my "flock of Jaguars" were startled. Indeed life was very good just then.

But lately things have not been going well. At the beginning of April Jaguars settled down at 1-1/16. Though I stood for hours at the club tape, my hair standing up on end and my eyeballs starting from their sockets, Jaguars still came through steadily at 1-1/16. To give them a chance of doing something, I left them alone for a whole week—with what agony you can imagine. Then I looked again; a whole week and anything might have happened. Pauper or millionaire? No, still 1-1/16.

Worse was to follow. Editors actually took to leaving out Jaguars altogether. I suppose they were sick of putting 1-1/16 in every edition. But how ridiculous it made my idea seem of watching them go up and down! How blank life became again!

And now what I dreaded most of all has happened. I have received a "Progress Report" from the mine. It gives the "total footage" for the month, special reference being made to "cross-cutting, winzing and sinking." The amount of "tons crushed" is announced. There is serious talk of "ore" being "extracted"; indeed there has already been a most alarming "yield in fine gold." In short, it can no longer be hushed up that the property may at any moment be "placed on a dividend-paying basis."

Probably I shall be getting a safe five per cent.!

"Dash it all," as I said to my solicitor this morning, "I might just as well have bought a rotten mortgage."

XVIII. THE THINGS THAT MATTER

Ronald, surveying the world from his taxi—that pleasant corner of the world, St. James's Park—gave a sigh of happiness. The blue sky, the lawn of daffodils, the mist of green upon the trees, were but a promise of the better things which the country held for him. Beautiful as he thought the daffodils, he found for the moment an even greater beauty in the Gladstone bags at his feet. His eyes wandered from one to the other, and his heart sang to him, "I'm going away, I'm going away, I'm going away."

The train was advertised to go at 2.22, and at 2.20 Ronald joined the Easter holiday crowd upon the platform. A porter put down his luggage and was then swallowed up in a sea of perambulators and flustered parents. Ronald never saw him again. At 2.40, amidst some applause, the train came in.

Ronald seized a lost porter.

"Just put these in for me," he said. "A first smoker."

"All this lot yours, Sir?"

"The three bags—not the milk-cans," said Ronald.

It had been a beautiful day before, but when a family of sixteen which joined Ronald in his carriage was ruthlessly hauled out by the guard, the sun seemed to shine with a warmth more caressing than ever. Even when the train moved out of the station and the children who had been mislaid emerged from their hiding-places and were bundled in anywhere by the married porters, Ronald still remained splendidly alone. And the sky took on yet a deeper shade of blue.

He lay back in his corner, thinking. For a time his mind was occupied with the thoughts common to most of us when we go away—thoughts of all the things we have forgotten to pack. I don't think you could fairly have called Ronald over-anxious about clothes. He recognised that it was the inner virtues which counted; that a well-dressed exterior was nothing without some graces of mind or body. But at the same time he did feel strongly that, if you are going to stay at a house where you have never visited before, and if you are particularly anxious to make a good impression, it *is* a pity that an accident of packing should force you to appear at dinner in green knickerbockers and somebody else's velvet smoking-jacket.

Ronald couldn't help feeling that he had forgotten something. It wasn't the spare sponge; it wasn't the extra shaving-brush; it wasn't the second pair of bedroom slippers. Just for a moment the sun went behind a cloud as he wondered if he had included the reserve razor-strop; but no, he distinctly remembered packing that.

The reason for his vague feeling of unrest was this. He had been interrupted while getting ready that afternoon; and, as he left whatever he had been doing in order to speak to his housekeeper, he had said to himself, "If you're not careful, you'll forget about that when you come back." And now he could not remember what it was he had been doing, nor whether he *had* in the end forgotten to go on with it. Was he selecting his ties, or brushing his hair, or——

The country was appearing field by field; the train rushed through cuttings gay with spring flowers; blue was the sky between the baby clouds ... but it all missed Ronald. What *could* he have forgotten?

He went over the days that were coming; he went through all the changes of toilet that the hours might bring. He had packed this and this and this and this—he was all right for the evening. Supposing they played golf?... He was all right for golf. He might want to ride.... He would be able to ride. It was too early for lawn tennis, but ... well, anyhow, he had put in flannels.

As he considered all the possible clothes that he might want, it really seemed that he had provided for everything. If he liked he could go to church on Friday morning; hunt otters from twelve to one on Saturday; toboggan or dig for badgers on Monday. He had the different suits necessary for those who attend a water-polo meeting, who play chess, or who go out after moths with a pot of treacle. And even, in the last resort, he could go to bed.

Yes, he was all right. He had packed *everything*; moreover, his hair was brushed and he had no smut upon his face. With a sigh of relief he lowered the window and his soul drank in the beautiful afternoon. "We are going away—we are going away—we are going away," sang the train.

At the prettiest of wayside stations the train stopped and Ronald got out. There were horses to meet him. "Better than a car," thought Ronald, "on an afternoon like this." The luggage was collected. "Nothing left out," he chuckled to himself, and was seized with an insane desire to tell the coachman so; and then they drove off through the fresh green hedgerows, Ronald trying hard not to cheer.

His host was at the door as they arrived. Ronald, as happy as a child, jumped out and shook him warmly by the hand, and told him what a heavenly day it was; receiving with smiles of pleasure the news in return that it was almost like summer.

"You're just in time for tea. Really, we might have it in the garden."

"By Jove, we might," said Ronald, beaming.

However, they had it in the hall, with the doors wide open. Ronald, sitting lazily with his legs stretched out and a cup of tea in his hands, and feeling already on the friendliest terms with everybody, wondered again at the difference which the weather could make to one's happiness.

"You know," he said to the girl on his right, "on a day like this, *nothing* seems to matter."

And then suddenly he knew that he was wrong, for he had discovered what it was which he had told himself not to forget ... what it was which he had indeed forgotten.

And suddenly the birds stopped singing and there was a bitter chill in the air.

And the sun went violently out.

He was wearing only half-a-pair of spats.

THREE STORIES

XIX. THE MAKING OF A CHRISTMAS STORY

Yuletide!

London at Yuletide!

A mantle of white lay upon the Embankment, where our story opens, gleaming and glistening as it caught the rays of the cold December sun; an embroidery of white fringed the trees; and under a canopy of white the proud palaces of Savoy and Cecil reared their silent heads. The mighty river in front was motionless, for the finger of Death had laid its icy hand upon it. Above—the hard blue sky stretching to eternity; below—the white purity of innocence. London in the grip of winter!

(Editor. *Come, I like this. This is going to be good. A cold day was it not?*

Author. *Very.*)

All at once the quiet of the morning was disturbed. In the distance a bell rang out, sending a joyous pæan to the heavens. Another took up the word, and then another, and another. Westminster caught the message from Bartholomew the son of Thunder, and flung it to Giles Without, who gave it gently to Andrew by the Wardrobe. Suddenly the air was filled with bells, all chanting together of peace and happiness, mirth and jollity—a frenzy of bells.

The Duke, father of four fine children, waking in his Highland castle, heard and smiled as he thought of his little ones....

The Merchant Prince, turning over in his magnificent residence, heard, and turned again to sleep, with love for all mankind in his heart....

The Pauper in his workhouse, up betimes, heard, and chuckled at the prospect of his Christmas dinner....

And, on the Embankment, Robert Hardrow, with a cynical smile on his lips, listened to the splendid irony of it.

(Editor. *We really are getting to the story now, are we not?*

Author. *That was all local colour. I want to make it quite clear that it was Christmas.*

Editor. *Yes, yes, quite so. This is certainly a Christmas story. I think I shall like Robert, do you know?*)

It was Christmas day, so much at least was clear to him. With that same cynical smile on his lips, he pulled his shivering rags about him, and half unconsciously felt at the growth of beard about his chin. Nobody would recognise him now. His friends (as he had thought them) would pass by without a glance for the poor outcast near them. The women that he had known would draw their skirts away from him in horror. Even Lady Alice——

Lady Alice! The cause of it all!

His thoughts flew back to that last scene, but twenty-four hours ago, when they had parted for ever. As he had entered the hall he had half wondered to himself if there could be anybody in the world that day happier than himself. Tall, well-connected, a vice-president of the Tariff Reform League, and engaged to the sweetest girl in England, he had been the envy of all. Little did he think that that very night he was to receive his *congé!*

What mattered it now how or why they had quarrelled? A few hasty words, a bitter taunt, tears, and then the end.

A last cry from her, "Go, and let me never see your face again!"

A last sneer from him, "I will go, but first give me back the presents I have promised you!"

Then a slammed door and—silence.

What use, without her guidance, to try to keep straight any more? Bereft of her love, Robert had sunk steadily. Gambling, drink, morphia, billiards, and cigars—he had taken to them all; until now in the wretched figure of the outcast on the Embankment you would never have recognised the once spruce figure of Handsome Hardrow.

(Editor. *It all seems to have happened rather rapidly, does it not? Twenty-four hours ago he had been*——

Author. *You forget that this is a* SHORT *story.*)

Handsome Hardrow! How absurd it sounded now! He had let his beard grow, his clothes were in rags, a scar over one eye testified——

(Editor. *Yes, yes. Of course, I quite admit that a man might go to the bad in twenty-four hours, but would his beard grow as*——

Author. *Look here, you've heard of a man going grey with trouble in a single night, haven't you?*

Editor. *Certainly.*

Author. *Well, it's the same idea as that.*

Editor. *Ah, quite so, quite so.*

Author. *Where was I?*

Editor. *A scar over one eye was just testifying—— I suppose he had two eyes in the ordinary way?*)

—testified to a drunken frolic of an hour or two ago. Never before, thought the policeman, as he passed upon his beat, had such a pitiful figure cowered upon the Embankment, and prayed for the night to cover him.

The——

He was——

Er—the——

(Editor. *Yes?*

Author. *To tell the truth, I am rather stuck for the moment.*

Editor. *What is the trouble?*

Author. *I don't quite know what to do with Robert for ten hours or so.*

Editor. *Couldn't he go somewhere by a local line?*

Author. *This is not a humorous story. The point is that I want him to be outside a certain house some twenty miles from town at eight o'clock that evening.*

Editor. *If I were Robert I should certainly start at once.*

Author. *No, I have it.*)

As he sat there, his thoughts flew over the bridge of years, and he was wafted on the wings of memory to other and happier Yuletides. That Christmas when he had received his first bicycle....

That Christmas abroad....

The merry house-party at the place of his Cambridge friend....

Yuletide at the Towers, where he had first met Alice!

Ah!

Ten hours passed rapidly thus....

(Author. *I put stars to denote the flight of years.*

Editor. *Besides, it will give the reader time for a sandwich.*)

Robert got up and shook himself.

(Editor. *One moment. This is a Christmas story. When are you coming to the robin?*

Author. *I really can't be bothered about robins just now. I assure you all the best Christmas stories begin like this nowadays. We may get to a robin later; I cannot say.*

Editor. *We must. My readers expect a robin, and they shall have it. And a wassail-bowl, and a turkey, and a Christmas-tree, and a*——

Author. *Yes, yes; but wait. We shall come to little Elsie soon, and then perhaps it will be all right.*

Editor. *Little Elsie. Good!*)

Robert got up and shook himself. Then he shivered miserably, as the cold wind cut through him like a knife. For a moment he stood motionless, gazing over the stone parapet into the dark river beyond, and as he gazed a thought came into his mind. Why not end it all— here and now? He had nothing to live for. One swift plunge, and— —

(Editor. *You forget. The river was frozen.*

Author. *Dash it, I was just going to say that.*)

But no! Even in this Fate was against him. *The river was frozen over!* He turned away with a curse....

What happened afterwards Robert never quite understood. Almost unconsciously he must have crossed one of the numerous bridges which span the river and join North London to South. Once on the other side, he seems to have set his face steadily before him, and to have dragged his weary limbs on and on, regardless of time and place. He walked like one in a dream, his mind drugged by the dull narcotic of physical pain. Suddenly he realised that he had left London behind him, and was in the more open spaces of the country. The houses were more scattered; the recurring villa of the clerk had given place to the isolated mansion of the stockbroker. Each residence stood in its own splendid grounds, surrounded by fine old forest trees and approached by a long carriage sweep. Electric——

(Editor. *Quite so. The whole forming a magnificent estate for a retired gentleman. Never mind that.*)

Robert stood at the entrance to one of these houses, and the iron entered into his soul. How different was this man's position from his own! What right had this man—a perfect stranger—to be happy and contented in the heart of his family, while he, Robert, stood, a homeless wanderer, alone in the cold?

Almost unconsciously he wandered down the drive, hardly realising what he was doing until he was brought up by the gay lights of the windows. Still without thinking, he stooped down and peered into the brilliantly lit room above him. Within all was jollity; beautiful women moved to and fro, and the happy laughter of children came to him. "Elsie," he heard some one call, and a childish treble responded.

(Editor. *Now for the robin.*

Author. *I am very sorry. I have just remembered something rather sad. The fact is that, two days before, Elsie had forgotten to feed the robin, and in consequence it had died before this story opens.*

Editor. *That is really very awkward. I have already arranged with an artist to do some pictures, and I remember I particularly ordered a robin and a wassail. What about the wassail?*

Author. *Elsie always had her porridge* UPSTAIRS.)

A terrible thought had come into Robert's head. It was nearly twelve o'clock. The house-party was retiring to bed. He heard the "Good-nights" wafted through the open window; the lights went out, to reappear upstairs. Presently they too went out, and Robert was alone with the darkened house.

The temptation was too much for a conscience already sodden with billiards, golf and cigars. He flung a leg over the sill and drew himself gently into the room. At least he would have one good meal, he too would have his Christmas dinner before the end came. He switched the light on and turned eagerly to the table. His eyes ravenously scanned the contents. Turkey, mince-pies, plum-pudding—all was there as in the days of his youth.

(Editor. *This is better. I ordered a turkey, I remember. What about the mistletoe and holly? I rather think I asked for some of them.*

Author. *We must let the readers take something for granted.*

Editor. *I am not so sure. Couldn't you say something like this: "Holly and mistletoe hung in festoons upon the wall?")*

Indeed, even holly and mistletoe hung in festoons upon the wall.

(Editor. *Thank you.*)

With a sigh of content Hardrow flung himself into a chair, and seized a knife and fork. Soon a plate liberally heaped with good things was before him. Greedily he set to work, with the appetite of a man who had not tasted food for several hours....

"Dood evening," said a voice. "Are you Father Kwistmas?"

Robert turned suddenly, and gazed in amazement at the white-robed figure in the doorway.

"Elsie," he murmured huskily.

(Editor. *How did he know? And why "huskily"?*

Author. *He didn't know, he guessed. And his mouth was full.*)

"Are you Father Kwistmas?" repeated Elsie.

Robert felt at his chin, and thanked Heaven again that he had let his beard grow. Almost mechanically he decided to wear the mask—in short, to dissemble.

"Yes, my dear," he said. "I just looked in to know what you would like me to bring you."

"You're late, aren't oo? Oughtn't oo to have come this morning?"

(Editor. *This is splendid. This quite reconciles me to the absence of the robin. But what was Elsie doing downstairs?*

Author. *I am making Robert ask her that question directly.*

Editor. *Yes, but just tell me now—between friends.*

Author. *She had left her golliwog in the room, and couldn't sleep without it.*

Editor. *I knew that was it.*)

"If I'm late, dear," said Robert, with a smile, "why, so are you."

The good food and wine in his veins were doing their work, and a pleasant warmth was stealing over Hardrow. He found to his surprise that airy banter still came easy to him.

"To what," he continued, "do I owe the honour of this meeting?"

"I came downstairs for my dolly," said Elsie. "The one you sent me this morning, do you remember?"

"Of course I do, my dear."

"And what have you bwought me now, Father Kwistmas?"

Robert started. If he was to play the rôle successfully he must find something to give her now. The remains of the turkey, a pair of finger-bowls, his old hat—all these came hastily into his mind, and were dismissed. He had nothing of value on him. All had been pawned long ago.

Stay! The gold locket studded with diamonds and rubies, which contained Alice's photograph. The one memento of her that he had kept, even when the pangs of starvation were upon him. He brought it from its resting-place next his heart.

"A little something to wear round your neck, child," he said. "See!"

"Thank oo," said Elsie. "Why, it opens!"

"Yes, it opens," said Robert moodily.

"Why, it's Alith! Sister Alith."

(Editor. *Ha!*

Author. *I thought you'd like that.*)

Robert leapt to his feet as if he had been shot.

"Who?" he cried.

"My sister Alith. Does oo know her too?"

Alice's sister! Heavens! He covered his face with his hands.

The door opened.

(Editor. *Ha again!*)

"What are you doing here, Elsie?" said a voice. "Go to bed, child. Why, who is this?"

"Father Kwithmath, thithter."

(Editor. *How exactly do you work the lisping?*

Author. *What do you mean? Don't children of Elsie's tender years lisp sometimes?*

Editor. *Yes, but just now she said "Kwistmas" quite correctly*——

Author. *I am glad you noticed that. That was an effect which I intended to produce. Lisping is brought about by placing the tongue upon the hard surface of the palate, and in cases where the subject is unduly excited or influenced by emotion the lisp becomes more pronounced. In this case*——

Editor. *Yeth, I thee.*)

"Send her away," cried Robert, without raising his head.

The door opened, and closed again. "Well," said Alice calmly, "and who are you? You may have lied to this poor child, but you cannot deceive me. You are *not* Father Christmas."

The miserable man raised his shamefaced head and looked haggardly at her.

"Alice!" he muttered, "don't you remember me?"

She gazed at him earnestly.

"Robert! But how changed!"

"Since we parted, Alice, much has happened."

"Yet it seems only yesterday that I saw you!"

(Editor. *It* WAS *only yesterday.*

Author. *Yes, yes. Don't interrupt now, please.*)

"To me it has seemed years."

"But what are you doing here?" said Alice.

"Rather, what are *you* doing here?" answered Robert.

(Editor. *I think Alice's question was the more reasonable one.*)

"I live here."

Robert gave a sudden cry.

"Your house! Then I have broken into your house! Alice, send me away! Put me in prison! Do what you will to me! I can never hold up my head again."

Lady Alice looked gently at the wretched figure in front of her.

"I am glad to see you again," she said. "Because I wanted to say that it was *my* fault!"

"Alice!"

"Can you forgive me?"

"Forgive you? If you knew what my life has been since I left you! If you knew into what paths of wickedness I have sunk! How only this evening, unnerved by excess, I have deliberately broken into this house—*your* house—in order to obtain food. Already I have eaten more than half a turkey and the best part of a plum pudding. I——"

With a gesture of infinite compassion she stopped him.

"Then let us forgive each other," she said with a smile. "A new year is beginning, Robert!"

He took her in his arms.

"Listen," he said.

In the distance the bells began to ring in the New Year. A message of hope to all weary travellers on life's highway. It was New Year's Day!

(Editor. *I thought Christmas Day had started on the Embankment. This would be Boxing Day.*

Author. *I'm sorry, but it must end like that. I must have my bells.*

Editor. *That's all very well. I have a good deal to explain as it is. Some of your story doesn't fit the pictures at all, and it is too late now to get new ones done.*

Author. *I am afraid I cannot work to order.*

Editor. *Yes, I know. The artist said the same thing. Well, I must manage somehow, I suppose. Good-bye. Rotten weather for August, isn't it?*)

XX. A MATTER-OF-FACT FAIRY TALE

Once upon a time there was a King who had three sons. The two eldest were lazy good-for-nothing young men, but the third son, whose name was Charming, was a delightful youth, who was loved by everybody (outside his family) who knew him. Whenever he rode through the town the people used to stop whatever work they were engaged upon and wave their caps and cry, "Hurrah for Prince Charming!"—and even after he had passed they would continue to stop work, in case he might be coming back the same way, when they would wave their caps and cry, "Hurrah for Prince Charming!" again. It was wonderful how fond of him they were.

But alas! his father the King was not so fond. He preferred his eldest son; which was funny of him, because he must have known that only the third and youngest son is ever any good in a family. Indeed, the King himself had been a third son, so he had really no excuse for ignorance on the point. I am afraid the truth was that he was jealous of Charming, because the latter was so popular outside his family.

Now there lived in the Palace an old woman called Countess Caramel, who had been governess to Charming when he was young. When the Queen lay dying, the Countess had promised her that she would look after her youngest boy for her, and Charming had often confided in Caramel since. One morning, when his family had been particularly rude to him at breakfast, Charming said to her:

"Countess, I have made up my mind, and I am going into the world to seek my fortune."

"I have been waiting for this," said the Countess. "Here is a magic ring. Wear it always on your little finger, and whenever you want help, turn it round once and help will come."

Charming thanked her and put the ring on his finger. Then he turned it round once just to make sure that it worked. Immediately the oddest little dwarf appeared in front of him.

"Speak and I will obey," said the dwarf.

Now Charming didn't want anything at all just then, so after thinking for a moment, he said, "Go away!"

The dwarf, a little surprised, disappeared.

"This is splendid," thought Charming, and he started on his travels with a light heart.

The sun was at its highest as he came to a thick wood, and in its shade he lay down to rest. He was awakened by the sound of weeping. Rising hastily to his feet he peered through the trees, and there, fifty yards away from him, by the side of a stream sat the most beautiful damsel he had ever seen, wringing her hands and sobbing bitterly. Prince Charming, grieving at the sight of beauty in such distress, coughed and came nearer.

"Princess," he said tenderly, for he knew she must be a Princess, "you are in trouble. How can I help you?"

"Fair Sir," she answered, "I had thought to be alone. But, since you are here, you can help me if you will. I have a—a brother——"

But Charming did not want to talk about brothers. He sat down on a fallen log beside her, and looked at her entranced.

"I think you are the most lovely lady in all the world," he said.

"Am I?" said the Princess, whose name, by the way, was Beauty.

She looked away from him and there was silence between them. Charming, a little at a loss, fidgeted nervously with his ring, and began to speak again.

"Ever since I have known you——"

"You are in need of help?" said the dwarf, appearing suddenly.

"Certainly not," said Charming angrily. "Not in the least. I can manage this quite well by myself."

"Speak, and I will obey."

"Then go away," said Charming; and the dwarf, who was beginning to lose his grip of things, again disappeared.

The Princess, having politely pretended to be looking for something while this was going on, turned to him again.

"Come with me," she said, "and I will show you how you can help me."

She took him by the hand and led him down a narrow glade to a little clearing in the middle of the wood. Then she made him sit down beside her on the grass, and there she told him her tale.

"There is a giant called Blunderbus," she said, "who lives in a great castle ten miles from here. He is a terrible magician, and years ago because I would not marry him he turned my—my brother into a—I don't know how to tell you—into a—a tortoise." She put her hands to her face and sobbed again.

"Why a tortoise?" said Charming, knowing that sympathy was useless, but feeling that he ought to say *something*.

"I don't know. He just thought of it. It—it isn't a very nice thing to be."

"And why should he turn your *brother* into it? I mean, if he had turned *you* into a tortoise—Of course," he went on hurriedly, "I'm very glad he didn't."

"Thank you," said Beauty.

"But I don't understand why——"

"He knew he could hurt me more by making my brother a tortoise than by making me one," she explained, and looked at him anxiously.

This was a new idea to Charming, who had two brothers of his own; and he looked at her in some surprise.

"Oh, what does it matter *why* he did it?" she cried, as he was about to speak. "Why do giants do things? *I* don't know."

"Princess," said Charming remorsefully, and kissed her hand, "tell me how I can help you."

"My brother," said Beauty, "was to have met me here. He is late again." She sighed and added, "He used to be *so* punctual."

"But how can I help him?" asked Charming.

"It is like this. The only way in which the enchantment can be taken off him is for some one to kill the Giant. But, if once the enchantment has stayed on for seven years, then it stays on for ever."

Here she looked down and burst into tears.

"The seven years," she sobbed, "are over at sundown this afternoon."

"I see," said Charming thoughtfully.

"Here is my brother," cried Beauty.

An enormous tortoise came slowly into view. Beauty rushed up to him and, having explained the situation rapidly, made the necessary introduction.

"Charmed," said the tortoise. "You can't miss the castle; it's the only one near here, and Blunderbus is sure to be at home. I need not tell you how grateful I shall be if you kill him. Though I must say," he added, "it puzzles me to think how you are going to do it."

"I have a friend who will help me," said Charming, fingering his ring.

"Well, I only hope you'll be luckier than the others."

"The others?" cried Charming in surprise.

"Yes; didn't she tell you about the others who tried?"

"I forgot to," said Beauty, frowning at him.

"Ah, well, perhaps in that case we'd better not go into it now," said the Tortoise. "But before you start I should like to talk to you privately for a moment." He took Charming on one side and whispered, "I say, do *you* know anything about tortoises?"

"Very little," said Charming. "In fact——"

"Then you don't happen to know what they eat?"

"I'm afraid I don't."

"Dash it, why doesn't *anybody* know? The others all made the most ridiculous suggestions. Steak and kidney puddings—shrimp sandwiches—and buttered toast. Dear me! The nights we had after the shrimp sandwiches! And the fool swore he had kept tortoises all his life!"

"If I may say so," said Charming, "I should have thought that *you* would have known best."

"The same silly idea they all have," said the Tortoise testily. "When Blunderbus put this enchantment on me, do you suppose he got a blackboard and a piece of chalk and gave me a lecture on the diet and habits of the common tortoise, before showing me out of the front gate? No, he simply turned me into the form of a tortoise and left my mind and soul as it was before. I've got the anatomy of a tortoise, I've got the very delicate inside of a tortoise, but I don't *think* like one, stupid. Else I shouldn't mind being one."

"I never thought of that."

"No one does, except me. And I can think of nothing else." He paused and added confidently. "We're trying rum omelettes just now. Somehow I don't think tortoises *really* like them. However, we shall see. I suppose you've never heard anything definite against them?"

"You needn't bother about that," said Charming briskly. "By to-night you will be a man again." And he patted him encouragingly on the shell and returned to take an affectionate farewell of the Princess.

As soon as he was alone, Charming turned the ring round his finger, and the dwarf appeared before him.

"The same as usual?" said the dwarf, preparing to vanish at the word. He was just beginning to get into the swing of it.

117

"No, no," said Charming hastily. "I really want you this time." He thought for a moment. "I want," he said at last, "a sword. One that will kill giants."

Instantly a gleaming sword was at his feet. He picked it up and examined it.

"Is this really a magic sword?"

"It has but to inflict one scratch," said the dwarf, "and the result is death."

Charming, who had been feeling the blade, took his thumb away hastily.

"Then I shall want a cloak of darkness," he said.

"Behold, here it is. Beneath this cloak the wearer is invisible to the eyes of his enemies."

"One thing more," said Charming. "A pair of seven-league boots.... Thank you. That is all to-day."

Directly the dwarf was gone, Charming kicked off his shoes and stepped into the magic boots; then he seized the sword and the cloak and darted off on his lady's behest. He had barely gone a hundred paces before a sudden idea came to him, and he pulled himself up short.

"Let me see," he reflected; "the castle was ten miles away. These are seven-league boots—so that I have come about two thousand miles. I shall have to go back." He took some hasty steps back, and found himself in the wood from which he had started.

"Well?" said Princess Beauty, "have you killed him?"

"No, n-no," stammered Charming, "not exactly killed him. I was just—just practising something. The fact is," he added confidently, "I've got a pair of new boots on, and——" He saw the look of cold surprise in her face and went on quickly, "I swear, Princess, that I will not return to you again without his head." He took a quick step in the direction of the castle and found himself soaring over it; turned eleven miles off and stepped back a pace; overshot it again, and arrived at the very feet of the Princess.

"His head?" said Beauty eagerly.

"I—I must have dropped it," said Charming, hastily pretending to feel for it. "I'll just go and——" He stepped off in confusion.

Eleven miles the wrong side of the castle, Charming sat down to think it out. It was but two hours to sundown. Without his magic boots he would get to the castle too late. Of course, what he really wanted to do was to erect an isosceles triangle on a base of eleven miles, having two sides of twenty-one miles each. But this was before Euclid's time.

However, by taking one step to the north and another to the southwest, he found himself close enough. A short but painful walk, with his boots in his hand, brought him to his destination. He had a moment's hesitation about making a first call at the castle in his stockinged feet, but consoled himself with the thought that in life-and-death matters one cannot bother about little points of etiquette, and that, anyhow, the giant would not be able to see them. Then, donning the magic cloak, and with the magic sword in his hand, he entered the castle gates. For an instant his heart seemed to stop beating, but the thought of the Princess gave him new courage....

The Giant was sitting in front of the fire, his great spiked club between his knees. At Charming's entry he turned round, gave a start of surprise, bent forward eagerly a moment, and then leant back chuckling. Like most over-grown men he was naturally kind-hearted and had a simple humour, but he could be stubborn when he liked. The original affair of the tortoise seems to have shown him both at his best and at his worst.

"Why do you walk like that?" he said pleasantly to Charming. "The baby is not asleep."

Charming stopped short.

"You see me?" he cried furiously.

"Of course I do! Really, you mustn't expect to come into a house without anything on your feet and not be a little noticeable. Even in a crowd I should have picked you out."

"That miserable dwarf," said Charming savagely, "swore solemnly to me that beneath this cloak I was invisible to the eyes of my enemies!"

"But then we aren't enemies," smiled the Giant sweetly. "I like you immensely. There's something about you—directly you came in.... I think it must be love at first sight."

"So *that's* how he tricked me!"

"Oh no, it wasn't really like that. The fact is you are invisible *beneath* that cloak, only—you'll excuse my pointing it out—there are such funny bits of you that aren't beneath the cloak. You've no idea how odd you look; just a head and two legs, and a couple of arms.... Waists," he murmured to himself, "are not being worn this year."

But Charming had had enough of talk. Griping his sword firmly, he threw aside his useless cloak, dashed forward, and with a beautiful lunge pricked his enemy in the ankle.

"Victory!" he cried, waving his magic sword above his head. "Thus is Beauty's brother delivered!"

The Giant stared at him for a full minute. Then he put his hands to his sides and fell back shaking in his chair.

"Her brother!" he roared. "Well, of all the—Her *brother!*" He rolled on the floor in a paroxysm of mirth. "Her brother! Oh you—You'll kill me! Her b-b-b-b-brother! Her b-b-b-b—her b-b-b—her b-b——"

The world suddenly seemed very cold to Charming. He turned the ring on his finger.

"Well?" said the Dwarf.

"I want," said Charming curtly, "to be back at home, riding through the streets on my cream palfrey, amidst the cheers of the populace.... At once."

An hour later Princess Beauty and Prince Udo, who was not her brother, gazed into each other's eyes; and Beauty's last illusion went.

"You've altered," she said slowly.

"Yes, I'm not really much like a tortoise," said Udo humorously.

"I meant since seven years ago. You're much stouter than I thought."

"Time hasn't exactly stood still with you, you know, Beauty."

"Yet you saw me every day, and went on loving me."

"Well,—er——" He shuffled his feet and looked away.

"*Didn't* you?"

"Well, you see—of course I wanted to get back, you see—and as long as you—I mean if we—if you thought we were in love with each other, then, of course, you were ready to help me. And so——"

"You're quite old and bald. I can't think why I didn't notice it before."

"Well, you wouldn't when I was a tortoise," said Udo pleasantly. "As tortoises go I was really quite a youngster. Besides, anyhow one never notices baldness in a tortoise."

"I think," said Beauty, weighing her words carefully, "I think you've gone off a good deal in looks the last day or two."

Charming was home in time for dinner, and the next morning he was more popular than ever outside his family as he rode through the streets of the city. But Blunderbus lay dead in his Castle. You and I know that he was killed by the magic sword; yet somehow a strange legend grew up around his death. And ever afterwards in that country, when one man told his neighbour a more than ordinarily humorous anecdote, the latter would cry, in between the gusts of merriment, "Don't! You'll make me die of laughter!" And then he would pull himself together, and add with a sigh, "Like Blunderbus."

XXI. THE SEASIDE NOVELETTE

[MAY BE READ ON THE PIER]

NO. XCVIII.—A SIMPLE ENGLISH GIRL

CHAPTER I

PRIMROSE FARM

Primrose Farm stood slumbering in the sunlight of an early summer morn. Save for the gentle breeze which played in the tops of the two tall elms all Nature seemed at rest. Chanticleer had ceased his song; the pigs were asleep; in the barn the cow lay thinking. A deep peace brooded over the rural scene, the peace of centuries. Terrible to think that in a few short hours ... but perhaps it won't. The truth is I have not quite decided whether to have the murder in this story or in No. XCIX.—The Severed Thumb. We shall see.

As her alarum clock (a birthday present) struck five, Gwendolen French sprang out of bed and plunged her face into the clump of nettles which grew outside her lattice window. For some minutes she stood there, breathing in the incense of the day; then dressing quickly she went down into the great oak-beamed kitchen to prepare breakfast for her father and the pigs. As she went about her simple duties she sang softly to herself, a song of love and knightly deeds. Little did she think that a lover, even at that moment, stood outside her door.

"Heigh-ho!" sighed Gwendolen, and she poured the bran-mash into a bowl and took it up to her father's room.

For eighteen years Gwendolen French had been the daughter of John French of Primrose Farm. Endowed by Nature with a beauty that is seldom seen outside this sort of story, she was yet as modest and as good a girl as was to be found in the county. Many a fine lady would have given all her Parisian diamonds for the peach-like complexion which bloomed on the fair face of Gwendolen. But the gifts of Nature are not to be bought and sold.

There was a sudden knock at the door.

"Come in," cried Gwendolen in surprise. Unless it was the cow, it was an entirely unexpected visitor.

A tall and handsome young man entered, striking his head violently against a beam as he stepped into the low-ceilinged kitchen.

"Good morning," he said, repressing the remark which came more readily to his lips. "Pray forgive this intrusion. The fact is I have lost my way, and I wondered whether you would be kind enough to inform me as to my whereabouts."

Gwendolen curtsied.

"This is Primrose Farm, Sir," she said.

"I fear," he replied with a smile, "it has been my misfortune never to have heard so charming a name before. I am Lord Beltravers of Beltravers Castle, Beltravers. Having returned last night from India I came out for an early stroll this morning, and I fear that I have wandered out of my direction."

"Why," cried Gwendolen, "your lordship is miles from Beltravers Castle. How tired and hungry you must be." She removed a lettuce from the kitchen-chair, dusted it, and offered it to him. (That is to say, the chair.) "Let me get you some milk," she added. Picking up a pail she went out to inspect the cow.

"Gad," said Lord Beltravers, as soon as he was alone. He paced rapidly up and down the tiled kitchen. "Deuce take it," he added recklessly, "she's a lovely girl." The Beltraverses were noted in two continents for their hard swearing.

"Here you are, Sir," said Gwendolen, returning with the precious liquid.

Lord Beltravers seized the pail and drained it at a draught.

"Heavens, but that was good!" he said. "What was it?"

"Milk," said Gwendolen.

"Milk, I must remember. And now may I trespass on your hospitality still further by trespassing on your assistance so far as to solicit your help in putting me far enough on my path to discover my way back to Beltravers Castle?" (When he was alone he said that sentence again to himself, and wondered what had happened to it.)

"I will show you," she said simply.

They passed out into the sunlit orchard. In an apple-tree a thrush was singing; the gooseberries were overripe; beet-roots were flowering everywhere.

"You are very beautiful," he said.

"Yes," said Gwendolen.

"I must see you again. Listen! To-night my mother, Lady Beltravers, is giving a ball. Do you dance?"

"Alas, not the Tango," she said sadly.

"The Beltraverses do not tang," he announced with simple dignity. "You valse? Good. Then will you come?"

"Thank you, my lord. Oh, I should love to!"

"That is excellent. And now I must bid you good-bye. But first, will you not tell me your name?"

"Gwendolen French, my lord."

"Ah! One 'f' or two?"

"Three," said Gwendolen simply.

CHAPTER II

BELTRAVERS CASTLE

Beltravers Castle was a blaze of lights. At the head of the old oak staircase (a magnificent example of the Selfridge period) the Lady Beltravers stood receiving her guests. Magnificently gowned in one of Rumpelmeyer's latest creations and wearing round her neck the famous Beltravers' seed-pearls, she looked the picture of stately magnificence. As each guest was announced by a bevy of footmen, she extended her perfectly-gloved hand, and spoke a few words of kindly welcome.

"Good evening, Duchess; so good of you to look in. Ah, Earl, charmed to meet you; you'll find some sandwiches in the billiard-room. Beltravers, show the Earl some sandwiches. How-do-you-do, Professor? Delighted you could come. Won't you take off your goloshes?"

All the county was there.

Lord Hobble was there wearing a magnificent stud; Erasmus Belt, the famous author, whose novel "Bitten: A Romance" went into two editions; Sir Septimus Root, the inventor of the fire-proof spat; Captain the Honourable Alfred Nibbs, the popular breeder of blood-goldfish—the whole world and his wife were present. And towering above them all stood Lord Beltravers of Beltravers Castle, Beltravers.

Lord Beltravers stood aloof in a corner of the great ball-room. Above his head was the proud coat-of-arms of the Beltraverses—a headless sardine on a field of tomato. As each new arrival entered Lord Beltravers scanned his or her countenance eagerly, and then turned

127

away with a snarl of disappointment. Would his little country maid never come?

She came at last. Attired in a frock which had obviously been created in Little Popley, she looked the picture of girlish innocence as she stood for a moment hesitating in the doorway. Then her eyes brightened as Lord Beltravers came towards her with long swinging strides.

"You're here!" he exclaimed. "How good of you to come. I have thought of you ever since this morning. There is a valse beginning. Will you valse it with me?"

"Thank you," said Gwendolen shyly.

Lord Beltravers, who valsed divinely, put his arm round her waist and led her into the circle of dancers.

CHAPTER III

AFFIANCED

The ball was at its height. Gwendolen, who had been in to supper eight times, placed her hand timidly on the arm of Lord Beltravers, who had just begged a polka of her.

"Let us sit this out," she said. "Not here—in the garden."

"Yes," said Lord Beltravers gravely. "Let us go. I have something to say to you."

Offering her his arm he led her down the great terrace which ran along the back of the house.

"How wonderful to have your ancestors always round you like this!" cooed Gwendolen, as she gazed with reverence at the two statues which fronted them.

"Venus," said Lord Beltravers shortly, "and Samson."

He led her down the steps and into the ornamental garden, and there they sat down.

"Miss French," said Lord Beltravers, "or if I may call you by that sweet name, 'Gwendolen,' I have brought you here for the purpose of making an offer to you. Perhaps it would have been more in accordance with etiquette had I approached your mother first."

"Mother is dead," said the girl simply.

"I am sorry," said Lord Beltravers, bending his head in courtly sympathy. "In that case I should have asked your father to hear my suit."

"Father is deaf," she replied. "He couldn't have heard it."

"Tut, tut," said Lord Beltravers impatiently; "I beg your pardon," he added at once, "I should have controlled myself. That being so," he went on, "I have the honour to make to you, Miss French, an offer of marriage. May I hope?"

Gwendolen put her hand suddenly to her heart. The shock was too much for her fresh young innocence. She was not *really* engaged to Giles Earwaker, though he too was hoping; and the only three times that Thomas Ritson had kissed her she had threatened to box his ears.

"Lord Beltravers," she began——

"Call me Beltravers," he begged.

"Beltravers, I love you. I give you a simple maiden's heart."

"My darling!" he cried, clasping her thumb impulsively. "Then we are affianced."

He slipped a ring off his finger and fitted it affectionately on two of hers.

"Wear this," he said gravely. "It was my mother's. She was a de Dindigul. See, this is their crest—a roeless herring over the motto '*Dans l'huile*'." Observing that she looked puzzled he translated the noble French words to her. "And now let us go in. Another dance is beginning. May I beg for the honour?"

"Beltravers," she whispered lovingly.

CHAPTER IV

EXPOSURE

The next dance was at its height. In a dream of happiness Gwendolen revolved with closed eyes round Lord Beltravers of Beltravers Castle, Beltravers.

Suddenly above the music rose a voice, commanding, threatening.

"Stop!" cried the Lady Beltravers.

As if by magic the band ceased and all the dancers were still.

"There is an intruder here," said Lady Beltravers in a cold voice. "A milkmaid, a common farmer's daughter. Gwendolen French, leave my house this instant!"

Dazed, hardly knowing what she did, Gwendolen moved forward. In an instant Lord Beltravers was after her. "No, mother," he said, with the utmost dignity. "Not a common milkmaid, but the future Lady Beltravers."

An indescribable thrill of emotion ran through the crowded ball-room. Lord Hobble's stud fell out; and Lady Susan Golightly hurried across the room and fainted in the arms of Sir James Batt.

"What!" cried the Lady Beltravers. "My son, the Last of the Beltraverses, the Beltraverses who came over with Julius Wernher (I should say Cæsar), marry a milkmaid?"

"No, mother. He is marrying what any man would be proud to marry—a simple English girl."

There was a cheer, instantly suppressed, from a Socialist in the band.

For just a moment words failed the Lady Beltravers. Then she sank into a chair, and waved her guests away.

"The ball is over," she said slowly. "Leave me. My son and I must be alone."

One by one, with murmured thanks for a delightful evening, the guests trooped out. Soon mother and son were alone. Lord Beltravers, gazing out of the window, saw the 'cellist laboriously dragging his 'cello across the park.

CHAPTER V

WEDDED

[And now, dear readers, I am in a difficulty. How shall the story go on? The editor of *The Seaside Library* asks quite frankly for a murder. His idea was that the Lady Beltravers should be found dead in the park next morning and that Gwendolen should be arrested. This seems to me both crude and vulgar. Besides I want a murder for No. XCIX of the series—The Severed Thumb.

No, I think I know a better way out.]

Old John French sat beneath a spreading pear-tree and waited. Early that morning a mysterious note had been brought to him, asking for an interview on a matter of the utmost importance. This was the trysting-place.

"I have come," said a voice behind him, "to ask you to beg your daughter——"

"*I have come*" cried the Lady Beltravers, "*to ask you*——"

"I HAVE COME," shouted her ladyship, "TO——"

John French wheeled round in amazement. With a cry the Lady Beltravers shrank back.

"Eustace," she gasped—"Eustace, Earl of Turbot!"

"Eliza!"

"What are you doing here? I came to see John French."

"What?" he asked, with his hand to his ear.

She repeated her remark loudly several times.

"I am John French," he said at last. "When you refused me and married Beltravers I suddenly felt tired of Society; and I changed my name and settled down here as a simple farmer. My daughter helps me on the farm."

"Then your daughter is——"

"Lady Gwendolen Hake."

A beautiful double wedding was solemnised at Beltravers in October, the Earl of Turbot leading Eliza, Lady Beltravers, to the altar, while Lord Beltravers was joined in matrimony to the beautiful Lady Gwendolen Hake. There were many presents on both sides, which partook equally of the beautiful and the costly.

Lady Gwendolen Beltravers is now the most popular hostess in the county; but to her husband she always seems the simple English milkmaid that he first thought her. Ah!

OUT-OF-DOORS

XXII. THE FIRST OF SPRING

There may be gardeners who can appear to be busy all the year round—doing even in the winter, their little bit under glass. But for myself I wait reverently until the 22nd of March is here. Then, Spring having officially arrived, I step out on to the lawn and summon my head-gardener.

"James," I say, "the winter is over at last. What have we got in that big brown-looking bed in the middle there?"

"Well, Sir," he says, "we don't seem to have anything do we, like?"

"Perhaps there's something down below that hasn't pushed through yet?"

"Maybe there is."

"I wish you knew more about it," I say angrily; "I want to bed out the macaroni there. Have we got a spare bed, with nothing going on underneath?"

"I don't know, Sir. Shall I dig 'em up and have a look?"

"Yes, perhaps you'd better," I say.

Between ourselves, James is a man of no initiative. He has to be told everything.

However mention of him brings me to my first rule for young gardeners—

"Never sow Spring Onions and New Potatoes in the same bed."

I did this by accident last year. The fact is, when the onions were given to me, I quite thought they were young daffodils; a mistake any one might make. Of course I don't generally keep daffodils and potatoes together; but James swore that the hard round things were tulip bulbs. It is perfectly useless to pay your head-gardener half-a-crown a week if he doesn't know the difference between potatoes and tulip bulbs. Well, anyhow, there they were, in the Herbaceous Border together, and they grew up side by side; the onions getting stronger every day, and the potatoes more sensitive. At last, just when they were ripe for picking, I found that the young onions had actually brought tears to the eyes of the potatoes—to such an extent that the latter were too damp for baking or roasting, and had to be mashed. Now, as everybody knows, mashed potatoes are beastly.

THE RHUBARB BORDER gives me more trouble than all the rest of the garden. I started it a year ago with the idea of keeping the sun off the young carnations. It acted excellently, and the complexion of the flowers improved tenfold. Then one day I discovered James busily engaged in pulling up the rhubarb.

"What are you doing?" I cried. "Do you want the young carnations to go all brown?"

"I was going to send some in to the cook," he grumbled.

"To the cook! What do you mean? Rhubarb isn't a vegetable."

"No, it's a fruit."

I looked at James anxiously. He had a large hat on, and the sun couldn't have got to the back of his neck.

"My dear James," I said, "I don't pay you half-a-crown a week for being funny. Perhaps we had better make it two shillings in future."

However, he persisted in his theory that in the spring people stewed rhubarb in tarts, and ate it!

Well, I have discovered since that this is actually so. People really do grow it in their gardens, not with the idea of keeping the sun off the young carnations, but under the impression that it is a fruit. Consequently I have found it necessary to adopt a firm line with my friends' rhubarb. On arriving at any house for a visit, the first thing I say to my host is, "May I see your rhubarb bed? I have heard such a lot about it."

"By all means," he says, feeling rather flattered, and leads the way into the garden.

"What a glorious sunset," I say, pointing to the west.

"Isn't it?" he says, turning round; and then I surreptitiously drop a pint of weed-killer on the bed.

Next morning I get up early and paint the roots of the survivors with iodine.

Once my host, who for some reason had got up early too, discovered me.

"What are you doing?" he asked.

"Just painting the roots with iodine," I said, "to prevent the rhubarb falling out."

"To prevent what?"

"To keep the green fly away," I corrected myself. "It's the new French intensive system."

But he was suspicious, and I had to leave two or three stalks untreated. We had those for lunch that day. There was only one thing for a self-respecting man to do. I obtained a large plateful of the weed and emptied the sugar basin and cream jug over it. Then I took a mouthful of the pastry, gave a little start, and said, "Oh, is this rhubarb? I'm sorry, I didn't know." Whereupon I pushed my plate away and started on the cheese.

ASPARAGUS

Asparagus wants watching very carefully. It requires to be tended like a child. Frequently I wake up in the middle of the night and wonder if James has remembered to put the hot-water bottle in the asparagus bed. Whenever I get up to look I find that he has forgotten.

He tells me to-day that he is beginning to think that the things which are coming up now are not asparagus after all, but young hyacinths. This is very annoying. I am inclined to fancy that James is not the man he was. For the sake of his reputation in the past I hope he is not.

POTTING OUT

I have spent a very busy morning potting out the nasturtiums. We have them in three qualities, mild, medium, and full. Nasturtiums are extremely peppery flowers, and take offence so quickly that the utmost tact is required to pot them successfully. In a general way all the red or reddish flowers should be potted as soon as they are old enough to stand it, but it is considered bad form among horticulturists to pot the white.

James has been sowing the roses. I wanted all the pink ones in one bed, and all the yellow ones in another, and so on; but James says

138

you never can tell for certain what colour a flower is going to be until it comes up. Of course, any fool could tell then.

"You should go by the picture on the outside of the packet," I said.

"They're very misleading," said James.

"Anyhow, they must be all brothers in the same packet."

"You might have a brother with red hair," says James.

I hadn't thought of that.

GRAFTING

Grafting is when you try short approaches over the pergola in somebody else's garden, and break the best tulip. You mend it with a ha'penny stamp and hope that nobody will notice; at any rate not until you have gone away on the Monday. Of course in your own garden you never want to graft.

I hope, at some future time to be allowed—even encouraged—to refer to such things as The Most Artistic Way to Frame Cucumbers, How to Stop Tomatoes Blushing (the homœopathic method of putting them next to the French beans is now discredited), and Spring Fashions in Fox Gloves. But for the moment I have said enough. The great thing to remember in gardening is that flowers, fruits and vegetables alike can only be cultivated with sympathy. Special attention should be given to backward and delicate plants. They should be encouraged to make the most of themselves. Never forget that flowers, like ourselves, are particular about the company they keep. If a hyacinth droops in the celery bed, put it among the pansies.

But above all, mind, a firm hand with the rhubarb.

XXIII. THE COMING OF THE CROCUS

"It's a bootiful day again, Sir," said my gardener, James, looking in at the study window.

"Bootiful, James, bootiful," I said, as I went on with my work.

"You might almost say as Spring was here at last, like."

"Cross your fingers quickly, James, and touch wood. Look here, I'll be out in a minute and give you some orders, but I'm very busy just now."

"Thought you'd like to know there's eleven crocuses in the front garden."

"Then send them away—we've got nothing for them."

"Crocuses," shouted James.

I jumped up eagerly and climbed through the window.

"My dear man," I said, shaking him warmly by the hand, "this is indeed a day. Crocuses! And in the front gar—on the South Lawn! Let us go and gaze at them."

There they were—eleven of them. Six golden ones, four white, and a little mauve chap.

"This is a triumph for you, James. It's wonderful. Has anything like this ever happened to you before?"

"There'll be some more up to-morrow, I won't say as not."

"Those really are growing, are they? You haven't been pushing them in from the top? They were actually born on the estate?"

"There'll be a fine one in the back bed soon," said James proudly.

"In the back—my dear James! In the spare bed on the North-east terrace, I suppose you mean? And what have we done in the Dutch Ornamental Garden?"

"If I has to look after ornamental gardens and South aspics and all, I ought to have my salary raised," said James, still harping on his one grievance.

"By all means raise some celery," I said coldly. "Take the spade and raise some for lunch. I shall be only too delighted."

"This here isn't the season for celery, as you know well. This here's the season for crocuses, as any one can see if they use their eyes."

"James, you're right. Forgive me. It is no day for quarrelling."

It was no day for working either. The sun shone upon the close-cropped green of the deer park, the sky was blue above the rose garden, in the tapioca grove a thrush was singing. I walked up and down my estate and drank in the good fresh air.

"James!" I called to my head-gardener.

"What is it now?" he grumbled.

"Are there no daffodils, to take the winds of March with beauty?"

"There's these eleven croc——"

"But there should be daffodils, too. Is not this March?"

"It may be March, but 'tisn't the time for daffodils—not on three shillings a week."

"Do you only get three shillings a week? I thought it was three shillings an hour."

"Likely an hour!"

"Ah well, I knew it was three shillings. Do you know, James, in the Scilly Islands there are fields and fields and fields of nodding daffodils out now."

"Lor'!" said James.

"Did you say 'lor' or 'liar'?" I asked suspiciously.

"To think of that now," said James cautiously.

He wandered off to the tapioca grove, leant against it in thought for a moment, and came back to me.

"What's wrong with this little bit of garden—this here park," he began, "is the soil. It's no soil for daffodils. Now what daffodils like is clay."

"Then for heaven's sake get them some clay. Spare no expense. Get them anything they fancy."

"It's too alloovial—that's what's the matter. Too alloovial. Now crocuses like a bit of alloovial. That's where you have it."

The matter with James is that he hasn't enough work to do. The rest of the staff is so busily employed that it is hardly ever visible. William, for instance, is occupied entirely with what I might call the poultry; it is his duty, in fact, to see that there are always enough ants' eggs for the gold-fish. All these prize Leghorns you hear about are the merest novices compared with William's *protegées*. Then John looks after the staggery; Henry works the coloured fountain;

and Peter paints the peacocks' tails. This keeps them all busy, but James is for ever hanging about.

"Almost seems as if they were yooman," he said, as we stood and listened to the rooks.

"Oh, are you there, James? It's a beautiful day. Who said that first? I believe you did."

"Them there rooks always make a place seem so home-like. Rooks and crocuses I say; and you don't want anything more."

"Yes; well, if the rooks want to build in the raspberry canes this year, let them, James. Don't be inhospitable."

"Course, some do like to see primroses, I don't say. But——"

"Primroses—I knew there was something. Where are they?"

"It's too early for them," said James hastily. "You won't get primroses now before April."

"Don't say 'now,' as if it were my fault. Why didn't you plant them earlier? I don't believe you know any of the tricks of your profession, James. You never seem to graft anything or prune anything, and I'm sure you don't know how to cut a slip. James, why don't you prune more? Prune now—I should like to watch you. Where's your pruning-hook? You can't possibly do it with a rake."

James spends most of his day with a rake—sometimes leaning on it, sometimes working with it. The beds are always beautifully kept. Only the most hardy annual would dare to poke his head up and spoil the smooth appearance of the soil. For those who like circles and rectangles of unrelieved brown, James is undoubtedly the man.

As I stood in the sun I had a brilliant idea.

"James," I said, "we'll cut the croquet lawn this afternoon."

"You can't play croquet to-day, it's not warm enough."

"I don't pay you to argue, but to obey. At the same time I should like to point out that I never said I was going to play croquet. I said that we, meaning you, would cut the lawn."

"What's the good of that?"

"Why, to encourage the wonderful day, of course. Where is your gratitude, man? Don't you want to do something to help? How can we let a day like this go past without some word of welcome? Out with the mower, and let us hail the passing of winter."

James looked at me in disgust.

"Gratitude!" he said indignantly to Heaven. "And there's my eleven crocuses in the front all a-singing together like anything on three bob a week!"

XXIV. THE LANDSCAPE GARDENER

Really I know nothing about flowers. By a bit of luck, James, my gardener, whom I pay half-a-crown a week for combing the beds, knows nothing about them either; so my ignorance remains undiscovered. But in other people's gardens I have to make something of an effort to keep up appearances. Without flattering myself I may say that I have acquired a certain manner; I give the impression of the garden lover, or the man with shares in a seed-company, or—or something.

For instance, at Creek Cottage, Mrs. Atherley will say to me, "That's an *Amphilobertus Gemini*," pointing to something which I hadn't noticed behind a rake.

"I am not a bit surprised," I say calmly.

"And a *Gladiophinium Banksii* next to it."

"I suspected it," I confess in a hoarse whisper.

Towards flowers whose names I know I adopt a different tone.

"Aren't you surprised to see daffodils out so early?" says Mrs. Atherley with pride.

"There are lots out in London," I mention casually. "In the shops."

"So there are grapes," says Miss Atherley.

"I was not talking about grapes," I reply stiffly.

However at Creek Cottage just now I can afford to be natural; for it is not gardening which comes under discussion these days, but landscape-gardening, and any one can be an authority on that. The

Atherleys, fired by my tales of Sandringham, Chatsworth, Arundel, and other places where I am constantly spending the week-end, are re-adjusting their two-acre field. In future it will not be called "the garden," but "the grounds."

I was privileged to be shown over the grounds on my last visit to Creek Cottage.

"Here," said Mrs. Atherley, "we are having a plantation. It will keep the wind off; and we shall often sit here in the early days of summer. That's a weeping ash in the middle. There's another one over there. They'll be lovely, you know."

"What's that?" I asked, pointing to a bit of black stick on the left; which, even more than the other trees, gave the impression of having been left there by the gardener while he went for his lunch.

"That's a weeping willow."

"This is rather a tearful corner of the grounds," apologised Miss Atherley. "We'll show you something brighter directly. Look there— that's the oak in which King Charles lay hid. At least, it will be when it's grown a bit."

"Let's go on to the shrubbery," said Mrs. Atherley. "We are having a new grass path from here to the shrubbery. It's going to be called Henry's Walk."

Miss Atherley has a small brother called Henry. Also there were eight Kings of England called Henry. Many a time and oft one of those nine Henrys has paced up and down this grassy walk, his head bent, his hands clasped behind his back; while behind his furrowed brow, who shall say what world-schemes were hatching? Is it the thought of Wolsey which makes him frown—or is he wondering where he left his catapult? Ah! who can tell us? Let us leave a veil of mystery over it ... for the sake of the next visitor.

"The shrubbery," said Mrs. Atherley proudly, waving her hand at a couple of laurel bushes, and a—I've forgotten its name now, but it is one of the few shrubs I really know.

"And if you're a gentleman," said Miss Atherley, "and want to get asked here again, you'll always *call* it the shrubbery."

"Really, I don't see what else you could call it," I said, wishing to be asked down again.

"The patch."

"True," I said. "I mean, Nonsense."

I was rather late for breakfast next morning; a pity on such a lovely spring day.

"I'm so sorry," I began, "but I was looking at the shrubbery from my window and I quite forgot the time."

"Good," said Miss Atherley.

"I must thank you for putting me in such a perfect room for it," I went on, warming to my subject. "One can actually see the shrubs— er—shrubbing. The plantation too seems a little thicker to me than yesterday."

"I expect it is."

"In fact, the tennis lawn——" I looked round anxiously. I had a sudden fear that it might be the new deer-park. "It still is the tennis lawn?" I asked.

"Yes. Why, what about it?"

"I was only going to say the tennis lawn had quite a lot of shadows on it. Oh, there's no doubt that the plantation is really asserting itself."

Eleven o'clock found me strolling in the grounds with Miss Atherley.

"You know," I said, as we paced Henry's Walk together, "the one thing the plantation wants is for a bird to nest in it. That is the hallmark of a plantation."

"It's Mother's birthday to-morrow. Wouldn't it be a lovely surprise for her?"

"It would indeed. Unfortunately this is a matter in which you require the co-operation of a feathered friend."

"Couldn't you try to persuade a bird to build a nest in the weeping ash? Just for this once."

"You're asking me a very difficult thing," I said doubtfully. "Anything else I would do cheerfully for you; but to dictate to a bird on such a very domestic affair—— No, I'm afraid I must refuse."

"It need only just begin to build one," pleaded Miss Atherley, "because Mother's going up town by your train to-morrow. As soon as she's out of the house the bird can go back to anywhere else it likes better."

"I will put that to any bird I see to-day," I said, "but I am doubtful."

"Oh, well," sighed Miss Atherley, "never mind."

"What do you think?" cried Mrs. Atherley as she came in to breakfast next day. "There's a bird been nesting in the plantation!"

Miss Atherley looked at me in undisguised admiration. I looked quite surprised—I know I did.

"Well, well!" I said.

"You must come out afterwards and see the nest and tell me what bird it is. There are three eggs in it. I am afraid I don't know much about these things."

"I'm glad," I said thankfully. "I mean, I shall be glad to."

We went out eagerly after breakfast. On about the only tree in the plantation with a fork to it a nest balanced precariously. It had in it three pale-blue eggs splotched with light-brown. It appeared to be a black-bird's nest with another egg or two to come.

"It's been very quick about it," said Miss Atherley.

"Of our feathered bipeds," I said, frowning at her, "the blackbird is notoriously the most hasty."

"Isn't it lovely?" said Mrs. Atherley.

She was still talking about it as she climbed into the trap which was to take us to the station.

"One moment," I said, "I've forgotten something." I dashed into the house and out by a side door, and then sprinted for the plantation. I took the nest from the weeping and overweighted ash and put it carefully back in the hedge by the tennis-lawn. Then I returned more leisurely to the house.

If ever you want a job of landscape-gardening thoroughly well done, you can always rely upon me.

XXV. PAT-BALL

"You'll play tennis?" said my hostess absently. "That's right. Let me introduce you to Miss—er—um."

"Oh, we've met before," smiled Miss—I've forgotten the name again now.

"Thank you," I said gratefully. I thought it was extremely nice of her to remember me. Probably I had spilt lemonade over her at a dance, and in some way the incident had fixed itself in her mind. We do these little things, you know, and think nothing of them at the moment, but all the time——

"Smooth," said a voice.

I looked up and found that a pair of opponents had mysteriously appeared, and that my partner was leading the way on to the court.

"I'll take the right-hand side, if you don't mind," she announced. "Oh, and what about apologising?" she went on. "Shall we do it after every stroke, or at the end of each game, or when we say good-bye, or never? I get so tired of saying 'sorry.'"

"Oh, but we shan't want to apologise; I'm sure we're going to get on beautifully together."

"I suppose you've played a lot this summer?"

"No, not at all yet, but I'm feeling rather strong, and I've got a new racquet. One way and another, I expect to play a very powerful game."

Our male opponent served. He had what I should call a nasty swift service. The first ball rose very suddenly and took my partner on the side of the head. ("Sorry," she apologised. "It's all right," I said magnanimously.) I returned the next into the net; the third clean bowled my partner; and off the last I was caught in the slips. (*One, love.*)

"Will you serve?" said Miss—I wish I could remember her surname. Her Christian name was Hope or Charity or something like that; I know, when I heard it, I thought it was just as well. If I might call her Miss Hope for this once? Thank you.

"Will you serve?" said Miss Hope.

In the right-hand court I use the American service, which means that I never know till the last moment which side of the racquet is going to hit the ball. On this occasion it was a dead heat—that is to say, I got it in between with the wood; and the ball sailed away over beds and beds of the most beautiful flowers.

"Oh, is *that* the American service?" said Miss Hope, much interested.

"South American," I explained. "Down in Peru they never use anything else."

In the left-hand court I employ the ordinary Hampstead Smash into the bottom of the net. After four Hampstead Smashes and four Peruvian Teasers (*love, two*) I felt that another explanation was called for.

"I've got a new racquet I've never used before," I said. "My old one is being pressed; it went to the shop yesterday to have the creases taken out. Don't you find that with a new racquet you—er—exactly."

In the third game we not only got the ball over the net but kept it between the white lines on several occasions—though not so often as our opponents (*three, love*); and in the fourth game Miss Hope served gentle lobs, while I, at her request, stood close up to the net and defended myself with my racquet. I warded off the first two shots amidst applause (*thirty, love*), and dodged the next three (*thirty, forty*), but the last one was too quick for me and won the cocoanut with some ease. (*Game. Love, four.*)

"It's all right, thanks," I said to my partner; "it really doesn't hurt a bit. Now then, let's buck up and play a simply dashing game."

Miss Hope excelled herself in that fifth game, but I was still unable to find a length. To be more accurate, I was unable to find a shortness—my long game was admirably strong and lofty.

"Are you musical?" said my partner at the end of it. (*Five, love.*) She had been very talkative all through.

"Come, come," I said impatiently, "you don't want a song at this very moment. Surely you can wait till the end of the set?"

"Oh, I was only just wondering."

"I quite see your point. You feel that Nature always compensates us in some way, and that as——"

"Oh, no!" said Miss Hope in great confusion. "I didn't mean that at all."

She must have meant it. You don't talk to people about singing in the middle of a game of tennis; certainly not to comparative strangers who have only spilt lemonade over your frock once before. No, no. It was an insult, and it nerved me to a great effort. I discarded—for it was my serve—the Hampstead Smash; I discarded the Peruvian Teaser. Instead, I served two Piccadilly Benders from the right-hand court and two Westminster Welts from the left-hand. The Piccadilly Bender is my own invention. It can only be served from the one court, and it must have a wind against it. You deliver it with your back to the net, which makes the striker think that you have either forgotten all about the game, or else are apologising to the spectators for your previous exhibition. Then with a violent contortion you slue your body round and serve, whereupon your opponent perceives that you *are* playing, and that it is just one more ordinary fault into the wrong court. So she calls "Fault!" in a contemptuous tone and drops her racquet ... and then adds hurriedly, "Oh, no, sorry, it wasn't a fault, after all." That being where the wind comes in.

The Westminster Welt is in theory the same as the Hampstead Smash, but goes over the net. One must be in very good form (or have been recently insulted) to bring this off.

Well, we won that game, a breeze having just sprung up; and, carried away by enthusiasm and mutual admiration, we collected another. (*Five, two.*) Then it was Miss Hope's serve again.

"Good-bye," I said; "I suppose you want me in the forefront again?"

"Please."

"I don't mind *her* shots—the bottle of scent is absolutely safe; but I'm afraid he'll win another packet of woodbines."

Miss Hope started off with a double, which was rather a pity, and then gave our masculine adversary what is technically called "one to kill." I saw instinctively that I was the one, and I held my racquet ready with both hands. Our opponent, who had been wanting his tea for the last two games, was in no mood of dalliance; he fairly let himself go over this shot. In a moment I was down on my knees behind the net ... and the next moment I saw through the meshes a very strange thing. The other man, with his racquet on the ground, was holding his eye with both hands!

"Don't you think," said Miss Hope (*two, five—abandoned*) "that your overhead volleying is just a little severe?"

XXVI. TEN AND EIGHT

The only event of importance last week was my victory over Henry by ten and eight. If you don't want to hear about that, then I shall have to pass on to you a few facts about his motor-bicycle. You'd rather have the other? I thought so.

The difference between Henry and me is that he is what I should call a good golfer, and I am what everybody else calls a bad golfer. In consequence of this he insults me with offers of bisques.

"I'll have ten this time," I said, as we walked to the tee.

"Better have twelve. I beat you with eleven yesterday."

"Thank you," I said haughtily, "I will have ten." It is true that he beat me last time, but then owing to bad management on my part I had nine bisques left at the moment of defeat simply eating their heads off.

Henry teed up and drove a "Pink Spot" out of sight. Henry swears by the "Pink Spot" if there is anything of a wind. I use either a "Quo Vadis," which is splendid for going out of bounds, or an "Ostrich," which has a wonderful way of burying itself in the sand. I followed him to the green at my leisure.

"Five," said Henry.

"Seven," said I; "and if I take three bisques it's my hole."

"You must only take one at a time," protested Henry.

"Why? There's nothing in Baedeker about it. Besides, I will only take one at a time if it makes it easier for you. I take one, and that brings me down to six, and then another one and that brings me down to five, and then another one and that brings me down to four. There! And as you did the hole in five, I win."

"Well, of course, if you like to waste them all at the start——"

"I'm not wasting them, I'm creating a moral effect. Behold, I have won the first hole; let us be photographed together."

Henry went to the next tee slightly ruffled and topped his ball into the road. I had kept mine well this side of it and won in four to five.

"I shan't take any bisques here," I said. "Two up."

At the third tee my "Quo Vadis" darted off suddenly to the left and tried to climb the hill. I headed it off and gave it a nasty dent from behind when it wasn't looking, and with my next shot started it rolling down the mountains with ever-increasing velocity. Not until it was within a foot of the pin did it condescend to stop. Henry, who had reached the green with his drive and had taken one putt too many, halved the hole in four. I took a bisque and was three up.

The fourth hole was prettily played by both of us, and with two bisques I had it absolutely stiff. Unnerved by this, Henry went all out at the fifth and tried to carry the stream in two. Unfortunately (I mean unfortunately for him) the stream was six inches too broad in the particular place at which he tried to carry it. My own view is that he should either have chosen another place or else have got a narrower stream from somewhere. As it was I won in an uneventful six, and took with a bisque the short hole which followed.

"Six up," I pointed out to Henry, "and three bisques left. They're jolly little things, bisques, but you want to use them quickly. *Bisque dat qui cito dat.* Doesn't the sea look ripping to-day?"

"Go on," growled Henry.

"I once did a two at this hole," I said, as I teed my ball. "If I did a two now and took a bisque, you'd have to do it in nothing in order to win. A solemn thought."

At this hole you have to drive over a chasm in the cliffs. My ball made a bee line for the beach, bounced on a rock, and disappeared into a cave. Henry's "Pink Spot," which really seemed to have a chance of winning a hole at last, found the wind too much for it and followed me below.

"I'm in this cave," I said, when we had found Henry's ball; and with a lighted match in one hand and a niblick in the other I went in and tried to persuade the "Ostrich" to come out. My eighth argument was too much for it, and we reappeared in the daylight together.

"How many?" I asked.

"Six," he said, as he hit the top of the cliff once more, and shot back on to the beach.

I left him and chivied my ball round to where the cliffs are lowest; then I got it gradually on to a little mound of sand (very delicate work, this), took a terrific swing and fairly heaved it on to the grass. Two more strokes put me on to the green in twenty. I lit a pipe and waited for Henry to finish his game of rackets.

"I've played twenty-five," he shouted.

"Then you'll want some of my bisques," I said. "I can lend you three till Monday."

Henry had one more rally and then picked his ball up. I had won seven holes and I had three bisques with which to win the match. I was a little doubtful if I could do this, but Henry settled the question by misjudging yet again the breadth of the stream. What is experience if it teaches us nothing? Henry must really try to enlarge his mind about rivers.

"Dormy nine," I said at the tenth tee, "and no bisques left."

"Thank Heaven for that," sighed Henry.

"But I have only to halve one hole out of nine," I pointed out. "Technically I am on what is known as velvet."

"Oh, shut up and drive."

I am a bad golfer, but even bad golfers do holes in bogey now and then. In the ordinary way I was pretty certain to halve one of the nine holes with Henry, and so win the match. Both the eleventh and the seventeenth, for instance, are favourites of mine. Had I halved one of those, he would have admitted cheerfully that I had played good golf and beaten him fairly. But as things happened——

What happened, put quite briefly, was this. Bogey for the tenth is four. I hooked my drive off the tee and down a little gully to the left, put a good iron shot into a bunker on the right, and then ran down a hundred-yard putt with a niblick for a three. One of those difficult down-hill putts.

"Luck!" said Henry, as soon as he could speak.

"I've been missing those lately," I said.

"Your match," said Henry; "I can't play against luck like that."

It was true that he had given me ten bisques, but, on the other hand, I could have given him a dozen at the seventh and still have beaten him.

However, I was too magnanimous to point that out. All I said was, "Ten and eight."

And then I added thoughtfully, "I don't think I've ever won by more than that."

XXVII. AN INLAND VOYAGE

Thomas took a day off last Monday in order to play golf with me. For that day the Admiralty had to get along without Thomas. I tremble to think what would have happened if war had broken out on Monday. Could a Thomasless Admiralty have coped with it? I trow not. Even as it was, battleships grounded, crews mutinied, and several awkward questions in the House of Commons had to be postponed till Tuesday.

Something—some premonition of this, no doubt—seemed to be weighing on him all day.

"Rotten weather," he growled, as he came up the steps of the club.

"I'm very sorry," I said. "I keep on complaining to the secretary about it. He does his best."

"What's that?"

"He taps the barometer every morning, and says it will clear up in the afternoon. Shall we go out now, or shall we give it a chance to stop?"

Thomas looked at the rain and decided to let it stop. I made him as comfortable as I could. I gave him a drink, a cigarette, and *Mistakes with the Mashie*. On the table at his elbow I had in reserve *Faulty Play with the Brassy* and a West Middlesex Directory. For myself I wandered about restlessly, pausing now and again to read enviously a notice which said that C.D. Topping's handicap was reduced from 24 to 22. Lucky man!

At about half-past eleven the rain stopped for a moment, and we hurried out.

"The course is a little wet," I said apologetically, as we stood on the first tee, "but with your naval experience you won't mind that. By the way, I ought to warn you that this isn't all casual water. Some of it is river."

"How do you know which is which?"

"You'll soon find out. The river is much deeper. Go on—your drive."

Thomas won the first hole very easily. We both took four to the green, Thomas in addition having five splashes of mud on his face while I only had three. Unfortunately the immediate neighbourhood of the hole was under water. Thomas, the bounder, had a small heavy ball which he managed to sink in nine. My own, being lighter, refused to go into the tin at all, and floated above the hole in the most exasperating way.

"I expect there's a rule about it," I said, "if we only knew, which gives me the match. However, until we find that out, I suppose you must call yourself one up."

"I shall want some dry socks for lunch," he muttered, as he splashed off to the tee.

"Anything you want for lunch you can have, my dear Thomas. I promise you that you shall not be stinted. The next green is below sea level altogether, I'm afraid. The first in the water wins."

Honours, it turned out, were divided. I lost the hole, and Thomas lost his ball. The third tee having disappeared, we moved on to the fourth.

"There's rather a nasty place along here," I said. "The secretary was sucked in the other day, and only rescued by the hair."

Thomas drove a good one. I topped mine badly, and it settled down in the mud fifty yards off. "Excuse me," I shouted, as I ran quickly after it, and I got my niblick on to it, just as it was disappearing. It was a very close thing.

"Well," said Thomas, as he reached his ball, "that's not what I call a brassy lie."

"It's what we call a corkscrew lie down here," I explained. "If you haven't got a corkscrew you'd better dig round it with something, and then when the position is thoroughly undermined—Oh, good shot!"

Thomas had got out of the fairway in one, but he still seemed unhappy.

"My eye," he said, bending down in agony; "I've got about half Middlesex in it."

He walked round in circles saying strange nautical things, and my suggestions that he should (1) rub the other eye and (2) blow his nose suddenly were received ungenerously.

"Anything you'd like me to do with my ears?" he asked bitterly. "If you'd come and take some mud out for me, instead of talking rot——"

I approached with my handkerchief and examined the eye carefully.

"See anything?" asked Thomas.

"My dear Thomas, it's *full* of turf. We mustn't forget to replace this if we can get it out. What the secretary would say—There! How's that?"

"Worse than ever."

"Try not to think about it. Keep the *other* eye on the ball as much as possible. This is my hole, by the way. Your ball is lost."

"How do you know?"

"I saw it losing itself. It went into the bad place I told you about. It's gone to join the secretary. Oh, no, we got him out, of course; I keep forgetting. Anyhow, it's my hole."

"I think I shall turn my trousers up again," said Thomas, bending down to do so. "Is there a local rule about it?"

"No; it is left entirely to the discretion and good taste of the members. Naturally a little extra license is allowed on a very muddy day. Of course, if—Oh, I see. You meant a local rule about losing your ball in the mud? No, I don't know of one, unless it comes under the heading of casual land. Be a sportsman, Thomas, and don't begrudge me the hole."

The game proceeded, and we reached the twelfth tee without any further *contretemps*; save that I accidentally lost the sixth, ninth and tenth holes, and that Thomas lost his iron at the eighth. He had carelessly laid it down for a moment while he got out of a hole with his niblick, and when he turned round for it the thing was gone.

At the twelfth tee it was raining harder than ever. We pounded along with our coat-collars up and reached the green absolutely wet through.

"How about it?" said Thomas.

"My hole, I think, and that makes us all square."

"I mean how about the rain? And it's just one o'clock."

"Just as you like. Well, I suppose it is rather wet. All right, let's have lunch."

We had lunch. Thomas had it in the only dry things he had brought with him—an ulster and a pair of Vardon cuffs, and sat as near the fire as possible. It was still raining in torrents after lunch, and Thomas, who is not what I call keen about golf, preferred to remain before the fire. Perhaps he was right. I raked up an old copy of *Stumers with the Niblick* for him, and read bits of the Telephone Directory out aloud.

After tea his proper clothes were dry enough in places to put on, and as it was still raining hard, and he seemed disinclined to come out again, I ordered a cab for us both.

"It's really rotten luck," said Thomas, as we prepared to leave, "that on the one day when I take a holiday, it should be so beastly."

"Beastly, Thomas?" I said in amazement. "The *one* day? I'm afraid you don't play inland golf much?"

"I hardly ever play round London."

"I thought not. Then let me tell you that to-day's was the best day's golf I've had for three weeks."

"Golly!" said Thomas.

XXVIII. ONE OF OUR SUFFERERS

There is no question before the country of more importance than that of National Health. In my own small way I have made something of a study of it, and when a Royal Commission begins its enquiries, I shall put before it the evidence which I have accumulated. I shall lay particular stress upon the health of Thomson.

"You'll beat me to-day," he said, as he swung his club stiffly on the first tee; "I shan't be able to hit a ball."

"You should have some lessons," I suggested.

Thomson gave a snort of indignation.

"It's not that," he said. "But I've been very seedy lately, and——"

"That's all right; I shan't mind. I haven't played a thoroughly well man for a month, now."

"You know, I think my liver——"

I held up my hand.

"Not before my caddie, please," I said severely, "he is quite a child."

Thomson said no more for the moment but hit his ball hard and straight along the ground.

"It's perfectly absurd," he said with a shrug; "I shan't be able to give you a game at all. Well, if you don't mind playing a sick man——"

"Not if you don't mind being one," I replied, and drove a ball which also went along the ground, but not so far as my opponent's. "There!

I'm about the only man in England who can do that when he's quite well."

The ball was sitting up nicely for my second shot, and I managed to put it on the green. Thomson's, fifty yards farther on, was reclining in the worst part of a bunker which he had forgotten about.

"Well, really," he said, "there's an example of luck for you. Your ball——"

"I didn't do it on purpose," I pleaded. "Don't be angry with me."

He made two attempts to get out and then picked his ball up. We walked in silence to the second tee.

"This time," I said, "I shall hit the sphere properly," and with a terrific swing I stroked it gently into a gorse bush. I looked at the thing in disgust and then felt my pulse. Apparently I was still quite well. Thomson, forgetting about his liver, drove a beauty. We met on the green.

"Five," I said.

"Only five?" asked Thomson suspiciously.

"Six," I said, holing a very long putt.

Thomson's health had a relapse. He took four short putts and was down in seven.

"It's really rather absurd," he said, in a conversational way, as we went to the next tee, "that putting should be so ridiculously important. Take that hole, for instance. I get on the green in a perfect three; you fluff your drive completely and get on in—what was it?"

"Five," I said again.

"Er—five. And yet you win the hole. It is rather absurd, isn't it?"

"I've often thought so," I admitted readily. "That is to say, when I've taken four putts. I'm two up."

On the third tee Thomson's health became positively alarming. He missed the ball altogether.

"It's ridiculous to try to play," he said with a forced laugh. "I can't see the ball at all."

"It's still there," I assured him.

He struck at it again and it hurried off into a ditch.

"Look here," he said, "wouldn't you rather play the pro.? This is not much of a match for you."

I considered. Of course a game with the pro. would be much pleasanter than a game with Thomson, but ought I to leave him in his present serious condition of health? His illness was approaching its critical stage, and it was my duty to pull him through if I could.

"No, no," I said. "Let's go on. The fresh air will do you good."

"Perhaps it will," he said hopefully. "I'm sorry I'm like this, but I've had a cold hanging about for some days, and that on the top of my liver——"

"Quite so," I said.

The climax was reached at the next hole, when, with several strokes in hand, he topped his approach shot into a bunker. For my sake he tried to look as though he had meant to run it up along the ground, having forgotten about the intervening hazard. It was a brave effort to hide from me the real state of his health, but he soon saw that it was hopeless. He sighed and pressed his hand to his eyes. Then he held his fingers a foot away from him, and looked at them as if he were trying to count them correctly. His state was pitiable, and I felt that at any cost I must save him.

I did. The corner was turned at the fifth, where I took four putts.

"You aren't going to win *all* the holes," he said grudgingly, as he ran down his putt.

Convalescence set in at the sixth when I got into an impossible place and picked up.

"Oh, well, I shall give you a game yet," he said. "Two down."

The need for further bulletins ceased at the seventh hole, which he played really well and won easily.

"A-ha, you won't beat me by much," he said, "in spite of my liver."

"By the way, how is the liver?" I asked.

"Your fresh-air cure is doing it good. Of course it may come on again, but——" He drove a screamer. "I think I shall be all right," he announced.

"All square," he said cheerily at the ninth. "I fancy I'm going to beat you now. Not bad, you know, considering you were four up. Practically speaking, I gave you a start of four holes."

I decided that it was time to make an effort again, seeing that Thomson's health was now thoroughly re-established. Of the next seven holes I managed to win three and halve two. It is only fair to say, though (as Thomson did several times), that I had an extraordinary amount of good luck, and that he was dogged by ill-fortune throughout. But this, after all, is as nothing so long as one's health is above suspicion. The great thing was that Thomson's liver suffered no relapse; even though, at the seventeenth tee, he was one down and two to play.

And it was on the seventeenth tee that I had to think seriously how I wanted the match to end. Thomson at lunch when he has won is a very different man from Thomson at lunch when he has lost. The more I thought about it, the more I realised that I was in rather a happy position. If I won, I won—which was jolly; if I lost, Thomson won—and we should have a pleasant lunch.

However, as it happened, the match was halved.

"Yes, I was afraid so," said Thomson; "I let you get too long a start. It's absurd to suppose that I can give you four holes up and beat you. It practically amounts to giving you four bisques. Four bisques is about six strokes; I'm not really six strokes better than you."

"What about lunch?" I suggested.

"Good; and you can have your revenge afterwards." He led the way into the pavilion. "Now I wonder," he said, "what I can safely eat. I want to be able to give you *some* sort of a game this afternoon."

Well, if there is ever a Royal Commission upon the national physique I shall insist on giving evidence. For it seems to me that golf, far from improving the health of the country, is actually undermining it. Thomson, at any rate, since he has taken to the game, has never been quite fit.

XXIX. CHUM

It is Chum's birthday to-morrow and I am going to buy him a little whip for a present, with a whistle at the end of it. When I next go into the country to see him I shall take it with me and explain it to him. Two day's firmness would make him quite a sensible dog. I have often threatened to begin the treatment on my very next visit, but somehow it has been put off; the occasion of his birthday offers a last opportunity.

It is rather absurd, though, to talk of birthdays in connection with Chum, for he has been no more than three months old since we have had him. He is a black spaniel who has never grown up. He has a beautiful astrachan coat which gleams when the sun is on it; but he stands so low in the water that the front of it is always getting dirty, and his ears and the ends of his trousers trail in the mud. A great authority has told us that, but for three white hairs on his shirt (upon so little do class distinctions hang), he would be a Cocker of irreproachable birth. A still greater authority has sworn that he is a Sussex. The family is indifferent—it only calls him a Silly Ass. Why he was christened Chum I do not know; and as he never recognises the name it does not matter.

When he first came to stay with us I took him a walk round the village. I wanted to show him the lie of the land. He had never seen the country before and was full of interest. He trotted into a cottage garden and came back with something to show me.

"You'll never guess," he said. "Look!" and he dropped at my feet a chick just out of the egg.

I smacked his head and took him into the cottage to explain.

"My dog," I said, "has eaten one of your chickens."

Chum nudged me in the ankle and grinned.

"*Two* of your chickens," I corrected myself, looking at the fresh evidence which he had just brought to light.

"You don't want me any more?" said Chum, as the financial arrangements proceeded. "Then I'll just go and find somewhere for these two."

And he picked them up and trotted into the sun.

When I came out I was greeted effusively.

"This is a wonderful day," he panted, as he wriggled his body. "I didn't know the country was like this. What do we do now?"

"We go home," I said, and we went.

That was Chum's last day of freedom. He keeps inside the front gate now. But he is still a happy dog; there is plenty doing in the garden. There are beds to walk over, there are blackbirds in the apple-tree to bark at. The world is still full of wonderful things. "Why only last Wednesday," he will tell you, "the fishmonger left his basket in the drive. There was a haddock in it, if you'll believe me, for Master's breakfast, so of course I saved it for him. I put it on the grass just in front of his study window, where he'd be *sure* to notice it. Bless you, there's always *something* to do in this house. One is never idle."

And even when there is nothing doing he is still happy, waiting cheerfully upon events until they arrange themselves for his amusement. He will sit for twenty minutes opposite the garden bank, watching for a bumble bee to come out of its hole. "I saw him go in," he says to himself, "so he's bound to come out. Extraordinary interesting world." But to his inferiors (such as the gardener) he pretends that it is not pleasure but duty which keeps him. "Don't talk to me, fool. Can't you see that I've got a job on here?"

Chum has found, however, that his particular mission in life is to purge his master's garden of all birds. This keeps him busy. As soon as he sees a blackbird on the lawn he is in full cry after it. When he gets to the place and finds the blackbird gone he pretends that he was going there anyhow; he gallops round in circles, rolls over once or twice, and then trots back again. "You didn't *really* think I was such a fool as to try to catch a *blackbird*?" he says to us. "No, I was just taking a little run—splendid thing for the figure."

And it is just Chum's little runs over the beds which call aloud for firmness—which, in fact, have inspired my birthday present to him. But there is this difficulty to overcome first. When he came to live with us, an arrangement was entered into (so he says) by which one bed was given to him as his own. In that bed he could wander at will, burying bones and biscuits, hunting birds. This may have been so, but it is a pity that nobody but Chum knows definitely which is the bed.

"Chum, you bounder," I shout, as he is about to wade through the herbaceous border.

He takes no notice; he struggles through to the other side. But a sudden thought strikes him, and he pushes his way back again.

"Did you call me?" he says.

"How *dare* you walk over the flowers?"

He comes up meekly.

"I suppose I've done *something* wrong," he says, "but I can't *think* what."

I smack his head for him. He waits until he is quite sure I have finished and then jumps up with a bark, wipes his paws on my trousers and trots into the herbaceous border again.

"Chum!" I cry.

He sits down in it and looks all round him in amazement.

"My own bed!" he murmurs. "*Given* to me!"

I don't know what it is in him which so catches hold of you. His way of sitting, a reproachful statue, motionless outside the window of whomever he wants to come out and play with him—until you can bear it no longer, but must either go into the garden or draw down the blinds for one day; his habit when you *are* out, of sitting up on his back legs and begging you with his front paws to come and *do* something—a trick entirely of his own invention, for no one would think of teaching him anything; his funny nautical roll when he walks, which is nearly a swagger, and gives him always the air of having just come back from some rather dashing adventure; beyond all this there is still something. And whatever it is, it is something, which every now and then compels you to bend down and catch hold of his long silky ears, to look into his honest eyes and say——

"You silly old ass! You *dear* old *silly* old ass!"

XXX. "UNDER ENTIRELY NEW MANAGEMENT"

I know a fool of a dog who pretends that he is a Cocker Spaniel, and is convinced that the world revolves round him wonderingly. The sun rises so it may shine on his glossy morning coat; it sets so his master may know that it is time for the evening biscuit; if the rain falls it is that a fool of a dog may wipe on his mistress's skirts his muddy boots. His day is always exciting, always full of the same good thing; his night a repetition of his day, more gloriously developed. If there be a sacred moment before the dawn when he lies awake and ponders on life, he tells himself confidently that it will go on for ever like this—a life planned nobly for himself, but one in which the master and mistress whom he protects must always find a place. And I think perhaps he would want a place for me too in that life, who am not his real master but yet one of the house. I hope he would.

What Chum doesn't know is this: his master and mistress are leaving him. They are going to a part of the world where a fool of a dog with no manners is a nuisance. If Chum could see all the good little London dogs, who at home sit languidly on their mistress's lap, and abroad take their view of life through a muff much bigger than themselves; if he could see the big obedient dogs, who walk solemnly through the Park carrying their master's stick, never pausing in their impressive march unless it be to plunge into the Serpentine and rescue a drowning child, he would know what I mean. He would admit that a dog who cannot answer to his own name and pays but little more attention to "Down, idiot," and "Come here, fool," is not every place's dog. He would admit it, if he had time. But before I could have called his attention to half the good dogs I had marked out, he would have sat down beaming in front of a motor-car ... and then he would never have known what now he will know so soon—that his master and mistress are leaving him.

It has been my business to find a new home for him. It is harder than you think. I can make him sound lovable, but I cannot make him sound good. Of course I might leave out his doubtful qualities, and describe him merely asbeautiful and affectionate; I might ... but I couldn't. I think Chum's habitual smile would get larger, he would wriggle the end of himself more ecstatically than ever if he heard himself summed up as beautiful and affectionate. Anyway, I couldn't do it, for I get carried away when I speak of him and I reveal all his bad qualities.

"I am afraid he is a snob," I confessed to one woman of whom I had hopes. "He doesn't much care for what he calls the lower classes."

"Oh?" she said.

"Yes, he hates badly dressed people. Corduroy trousers tied up at the knee always excite him. I don't know if any of your family—no, I suppose not. But if he ever sees a man with his trousers tied up at the knee he goes for him. And he can't bear tradespeople; at least not the men. Washer-women he loves. He rather likes the washing-basket too. Once, when he was left alone with it for a moment, he appeared shortly afterwards on the lawn with a pair of—well, I mean he had no business with them at all. We got them away after a bit of a chase, and then they had to go to the wash again. It seemed rather a pity when they'd only just come back. Of course I smacked his head for him; but he looks so surprised and reproachful when he's done wrong that you never feel it's quite his fault."

"I doubt if I shall be able to take him after all," she said. "I've just remembered——"

I forget what it was she remembered, but it meant that I was still without a new home for Chum.

"What does he eat?" somebody else asked me. It seemed hopeful; I could see Chum already installed.

"Officially," I said, "he lives on puppy biscuits; he also has the toast-crusts after breakfast and an occasional bone. Privately he is fond of bees; I have seen him eat as many as six bees in an afternoon. Sometimes he wanders down to the kitchen-garden and picks the gooseberries; he likes all fruit, but gooseberries are the things he can reach best. When there aren't any gooseberries about, he has to be content with the hips and haws from the rose-trees. But really, you needn't bother, he can eat anything. The only thing he doesn't like is whitening. We were just going to mark the lawn one day, and while we were busy pegging it out he wandered up and drank the whitening out of the marker. It is practically the only disappointment he has ever had. He looked at us, and you could see that his opinion of us had gone down. 'What did you *put* it there for, if you didn't mean me to drink it?' he said reproachfully. Then he turned and walked slowly and thoughtfully back to his kennel. He never came out till next morning."

"Really?" said my man. "Well, I shall have to think about it. I'll let you know."

Of course, I knew what that meant.

With a third dog-lover to whom I spoke the negotiations came to grief, not apparently because of any faults of Chum's but because, if you will believe it, of my own shortcomings. At least, I can suppose nothing else. For this man had been enthusiastic about him. He had revelled in the tale of Chum's wickedness; he had adored him for being so conceited. He had practically said that he would take him.

"Do," I begged, "I'm sure he'd be happy with you. You see, he's not everybody's dog; I mean I don't want any odd man whom I don't know to take him. It must be a friend of mine, so that I shall often be able to see Chum afterwards."

"So that—what?" he asked anxiously.

"So that I shall often be able to see Chum afterwards. Week-ends, you know, and so on. I couldn't bear to lose the silly old ass altogether."

He looked thoughtful; and, when I went on to speak about Chum's fondness for chickens, and his other lovable ways, he changed the subject altogether. He wrote afterwards that he was sorry he couldn't manage with a third dog. And I like to think he was not afraid of Chum—but only of me.

But I have found the right man at last. A day will come soon when I shall take Chum from his present home to his new one. That will be a great day for him. I can see him in the train, wiping his boots effusively on every new passenger, wriggling under the seat and out again from sheer joy of life; I can see him in the taxi, taking his one brief impression of a world that means nothing to him; I can see him in another train joyous, eager, putting his paws on my collar from time to time and saying excitedly, "What a day this is!" And if he survives the journey; if I can keep him on the way from all delightful deaths he longs to try; if I can get him safely to his new house, then I can see him——

Well, I wonder. What will they do to him? When I see him again, will he be a sober little dog, answering to his name, careful to keep his muddy feet off the visitor's trousers, grown up, obedient, following to heel round the garden, the faithful servant of his master? Or will he be the same old silly ass, no use to anybody, always dirty, always smiling, always in the way, a clumsy, blundering fool of a dog who knows you can't help loving him? I wonder....

Between ourselves, I don't think they *can* alter him now.... Oh, I hope they can't.

XXXI. A FAREWELL TOUR

This is positively Chum's last appearance in print—for his own sake no less than for yours. He is conceited enough as it is, but if once he got to know that people are always writing about him in books his swagger would be unbearable. However, I have said good-bye to him now; I have no longer any rights in him. Yesterday I saw him off to his new home, and when we meet again it will be on a different footing. "Is that your dog?" I shall say to his master. "What is he? A Cocker? Jolly little fellows, aren't they? I had one myself once."

As Chum refused to do the journey across London by himself, I met him at Liverpool Street. He came up, in a crate; the world must have seemed very small to him on the way. "Hallo, old ass," I said to him through the bars, and in the little space they gave him he wriggled his body with delight. "Thank Heaven there's *one* of 'em alive," he said.

"I think this is my dog," I said to the guard, and I told him my name.

He asked for my card.

"I'm afraid I haven't one with me," I explained. When policemen touch me on the shoulder and ask me to go quietly; when I drag old gentlemen from underneath motor-'buses, and they decide to adopt me on the spot; on all the important occasions when one really wants a card, I never have one with me.

"Can't give him up without proof of identity," said the guard, and Chum grinned at the idea of being thought so valuable.

I felt in my pockets for letters. There was only one, but it offered to lend me £10,000 on my note of hand alone. It was addressed to

"Dear Sir," and though I pointed out to the guard that I was the "Sir," he still kept tight hold of Chum. Strange that one man should be prepared to trust me with £10,000, and another should be so chary of confiding to me a small black spaniel.

"Tell the gentleman who I am," I said imploringly through the bars, "Show him you know me."

"He's *really* all right," said Chum, looking at the guard with his great honest brown eyes. "He's been with us for years."

And then I had an inspiration. I turned down the inside pocket of my coat, and there, stitched into it, was the label of my tailor's with my name written on it. I had often wondered why tailors did this; obviously they know how stupid guards can be.

"I suppose that's all right," said the guard reluctantly. Of course I might have stolen the coat. I see his point.

"You—you wouldn't like a nice packing case for yourself?" I said timidly. "You see, I thought I'd put Chum on the lead. I've got to take him to Paddington, and he must be tired of his shell by now. It isn't as if he were *really* an armadillo."

The guard thought he would like a shilling and a nice packing case. Wood, he agreed, was always wood, particularly in winter, but there were times when you were not ready for it.

"How are you taking him?" he asked, getting to work with a chisel. "Underground?"

"Underground?" I cried in horror. "Take Chum on the Underground? Take—— Have you ever taken a large live conger-eel on the end of a string into a crowded carriage?"

182

The guard never had.

"Well, don't. Take him in a taxi instead. Don't waste him on other people."

The crate yawned slowly, and Chum emerged all over straw. We had an anxious moment, but the two of us got him down and put the lead on him. Then Chum and I went off for a taxi.

"Hooray," said Chum, wriggling all over, "isn't this splendid? I say, which way are you going? I'm going this way.... No, I mean the other way."

Somebody had left some of his milk-cans on the platform. Three times we went round one in opposite directions and unwound ourselves the wrong way. Then I hauled him in, took him, struggling, in my arms and got into a cab.

The journey to Paddington was full of interest. For a whole minute Chum stood quietly on the seat, rested his fore-paws on the open window and drank in London. Then he jumped down and went mad. He tried to hang me with the lead, and then in remorse tried to hang himself. He made a dash for the little window at the back; missed it and dived out of the window at the side, was hauled back and kissed me ecstatically in the eye with his sharpest tooth.... "And I thought the world was at an end," he said, "and there were no more people. Oh, I am an ass. I say, did you notice I'd had my hair cut? How do you like my new trousers? I must show you them." He jumped on to my lap. "No, I think you'll see them better on the ground," he said, and jumped down again. "Or no, perhaps you *would* get a better view if——" he jumped up hastily, "and yet I don't know——" he dived down, "though of course, if you—— Oh lor'! this *is* a day," and he put both paws lovingly on my collar.

Suddenly he was quiet again. The stillness, the absence of storm in the taxi, was so unnatural that I began to miss it. "Buck up, old fool," I said, but he sat motionless by my side, plunged in thought. I tried to cheer him up. I pointed out King's Cross to him; he wouldn't even bark at it. I called his attention to the poster outside Euston Theatre of The Two Biffs; for all the regard he showed he might never even have heard of them. The monumental masonry by Portland Road failed to uplift him.

At Baker Street he woke up, and grinned cheerily. "It's all right," he said, "I was trying to remember what happened to me this morning—something rather miserable, I thought, but I can't get hold of it. However it's all right now. How are *you*?" And he went mad again.

At Paddington I bought a label at the book-stall and wrote it for him. He went round and round my leg looking for me. "Funny thing," he said, as he began to unwind, "he was here a moment ago. I'll just go round once more. I rather think.... *Ow*! Oh, there you are!" I stepped off him, unravelled the lead and dragged him to the Parcels Office.

"I want to send this by the two o'clock train," I said to the man the other side of the counter.

"Send what?" he said.

I looked down. Chum was making himself very small and black in the shadow of the counter. He was completely hidden from the sight of anybody the other side of it.

"Come out," I said, "and show yourself."

"Not much," he said. "A parcel! I'm not going to be a jolly old parcel for anybody."

"It's only a way of speaking," I pleaded. "Actually you are travelling as a small black gentleman. You will go with the guard—a delightful man."

Chum came out reluctantly. The clerk leant over the counter and managed to see him.

"According to our regulations," he said, and I always dislike people who begin like that, "he has to be on a chain. A leather lead won't do."

Chum smiled all over himself. I don't know which pleased him more—the suggestion that he was a very large and fierce dog, or the impossibility now of his travelling with the guard, delightful man though he might be. He gave himself a shake and started for the door.

"Tut, tut, it's a great disappointment to me," he said, trying to look disappointed, but his back *would* wriggle. "This chain business— silly of us not to have known—well, well, we shall be wiser another time. Now let's go home."

Poor old Chum; I *had* known. From a large coat pocket I produced a chain.

"*Dash* it," said Chum, looking up at me pathetically, "you might almost *want* to get rid of me."

He was chained, and the label tied on to him. Forgive me that label, Chum; I think that was the worst offence of all. And why should I label one who was speaking so eloquently for himself; who said from the tip of his little black nose to the end of his stumpy black tail, "I'm a silly old ass, but there's nothing wrong in me, and they're sending me away!" But according to the regulations—one must obey the regulations, Chum.

I gave him to the guard—a delightful man. The guard and I chained him to a brake or something. Then the guard went away, and Chum and I had a little talk....

After that the train went off.

Good-bye, little dog.

XXXII. PHYSICAL CULTURE

"Why don't you sit up?" said Adela at dinner, suddenly prodding me in the back. Adela is old enough to take a motherly interest in my figure, and young enough to look extremely pretty while doing so.

"I always stoop at meals," I explained; "it helps the circulation. My own idea."

"But it looks so bad. You ought——"

"Don't improve me," I begged.

"No wonder you have——"

"Hush! I haven't. I got a bullet on the liver in the campaign of '03, due to over smoking; and sometimes it hurts me a little in the cold weather. That's all."

"Why don't you try the Hyperion?"

"I will. Where is it?"

"It isn't anywhere; you buy it."

"Oh, I thought you dined at it. What do you buy it for?"

"It's one of those developers with elastics and pulleys and so on. Every morning early, for half an hour before breakfast——"

"You *are* trying to improve me," I said suspiciously.

"But they are such good things," went on Adela earnestly. "They really do help to make you beautiful——"

"I *am* beautiful."

"Well, much more beautiful, and strong——"

"Are you being simply as tactful as you can be?"

"——and graceful."

"It isn't as though you were actually a relation," I protested.

Adela continued, full of her idea.

"It would do you so much good, you know. Would you promise me to use it every day if I sent you mine?"

"Why don't you want yours any more? Are you perfect now?"

"You can easily hook it to the wall——"

"I suppose," I reflected, "there is a limit of beauty beyond which it is dangerous to go. After that either the thing would come off its hook, or——"

"Well," said Adela suddenly, "aren't I looking well?"

"You're looking radiant," I said appreciatively; "but it may only be because you're going to marry Billy next month."

She smiled and blushed. "Well, I'll send it to you," she said. "And you try it for a week, and then tell me if you don't feel better. Oh, and don't do all the exercises to begin with; start with three or four of the easy ones."

"Of course," I said.

I undid the wrappings eagerly, took off the lid of the box, and was confronted with (apparently) six pairs of braces. I shook them out of the box and saw I had made a mistake. It was one pair of braces for Magog. I picked it up, and I knew that I was in the presence of the Hyperion. In five minutes I had screwed a hook into the bedroom wall and attached the beautifier. Then I sat on the edge of the bed and looked at it.

There was a tin plate fastened to the top, with the word "LADIES" on it. I got up, removed it with a knife, and sat down again. Everything was very dusty, and I wondered when Adela had last developed herself.

By-and-by I went into the other room to see if I had overlooked anything. I found on the floor a chart of exercises, and returned triumphantly with it.

There were thirty exercises altogether, and the chart gave you:

(1) A detailed explanation of how to do each particular exercise;

(2) A photograph of a lady doing it.

"After all," I reassured myself, after the first bashful glance, "it is Adela who has thrust this upon me; and she must have known." So I studied it.

Nos. 10, 15 and 28 seemed the easiest; I decided to confine myself to them. For the first of these you strap yourself in at the waist, grasp the handles, and fall slowly backwards until your head touches the floor—all the elastic cords being then at full stretch. When I had got very slowly halfway down, an extra piece of elastic which had got hitched somewhere came suddenly into play, and I did the rest of the journey without a stop, finishing up sharply against the towel-horse. The chart had said, "Inhale going down," and I was inhaling hard at the moment that the towel-horse and two damp towels spread themselves over my face.

"So much for Exercise 10," I thought, as I got up. "I'll just get the idea to-night, and then start properly to-morrow. Now for No. 15."

Somehow I felt instinctively that No. 15 would cause trouble. For No. 15 you stand on the right foot, fasten the left foot to one of the cords, and stretch it out as far as you can....

What—officially—you do then, I cannot say....

Some people can stand easily upon the right foot when the left is fastened to the wall ... others cannot.... It is a gift....

Having recovered from my spontaneous rendering of No. 15 I turned to No. 28. This one, I realised, was extremely important. I would do it twelve times.

You begin by lying flat on the floor roped in at the waist, and with your hands (grasping the elastic cords) held straight up in the air. The tension on your waist is then extreme but on your hands only moderate. Then taking a deep breath you pull your arms slowly out until they lie along the floor. The tension becomes terrific, the strain on every part of you is immense. While I lay there, taking a deep breath before relaxing, I said to myself, "The strain will be too much for me." I was wrong. It was too much for the hook. The hook whizzed out, everything flew at me at once, and I remembered no more....

As I limped into bed, I trod heavily upon something sharp. I shrieked and bent down to see what had bitten me. It was a tin plate bearing the word "LADIES."

"Well?" said Adela a week later.

I looked at her for a long time. "When did you last use the Hyperion?" I asked.

"About a year ago."

"Ah!... You don't remember the chart that went with it?"

"Not well. Except, of course, that each exercise was arranged for a particular object, according to what you wanted."

"Exactly. So I discovered yesterday. It was in very small type, and I missed it at first."

"Well, how many did you do?"

"I limited myself to exercises 10, 15 and 28. Do you happen to remember what those are for?"

"Not particularly."

"No. Well, I started with No. 10. No. 10 you may recall is one of the most perilous. I nearly died over No. 10. And when I had been doing it for a week I discovered what its particular object was."

"What?"

"*To round the forearm'!* Yes, madam," I said bitterly, "I have spent a week of agony ... and I have rounded one forearm."

"Why didn't you try another?"

"I did. I tried No. 15. Six times in the pursuit of No. 15 have I been shot up to the ceiling by the left foot ... and what for, Adela? *'To arch the instep'!* Look at my instep! Why should I *want* to arch it?"

"I wish I could remember which chart I sent you," said Adela, wrinkling her brow.

"It was the wrong one," I said....

There was a long silence.

"Oh," said Adela suddenly, "you never told me about No. 28."

"Pardon me," I said, "I cannot bear to speak of 28."

"Why, was it even more unsuitable than the other two?"

"I found, when I had done it six times that its object was stated to be, *'To remove double chin.'* That, however, was not the real effect. And, so I crossed out the false comment and wrote the true one in its place."

"And what is that?" asked Adela.

"*To remove the hook,*" I said gloomily.

XXXIII. AN INSURANCE ACT

Of course I had always known that a medical examination was a necessary preliminary to insurance, but in my own case I had expected the thing to be the merest formality. The doctor, having seen at a glance what a fine strong healthy fellow I was, would look casually at my tongue, apologise for having doubted it, enquire genially what my grandfather had died of, and show me to the door. This idea of mine was fostered by the excellent testimonial which I had written myself at the Company's bidding. "Are you suffering from any constitutional disease?—*No.* Have you ever had gout?—*No.* Are you deformed?—*No.* Are you of strictly sober and temperate habits?—- *No,* I mean *Yes.*" My replies had been a model of what an Assurance Company expects. Then why the need of a doctor?

However, they insisted.

The doctor began quietly enough. He asked, as I had anticipated, after the health of my relations. I said that they were very fit; and not to be outdone in politeness, expressed the hope that his people, too, were keeping well in this trying weather. He wondered if I drank much. I said, "Oh, well, perhaps I will," with an apologetic smile, and looked round for the sideboard. Unfortunately he did not pursue the matter....

"And now," he said, after the hundredth question, "I should like to look at your chest."

I had seen it coming for some time. In vain I had tried to turn the conversation—to lead him back to the subject of drinks or my relations. It was no good. He was evidently determined to see my chest. Nothing could move him from his resolve.

Trembling, I prepared for the encounter. What terrible disease was he going to discover?

He began by tapping me briskly all over in a series of double-knocks. For the most part one double-knock at any point appeared to satisfy him, but occasionally there would be no answer and he would knock again. At one spot he knocked four times before he could make himself heard.

"This," I said to myself at the third knock, "has torn it. I shall be ploughed," and I sent an urgent message to my chest. "For 'eving's sake do something, you fool. Can't you hear the gentleman?" I suppose that roused it, for at the next knock he passed on to an adjacent spot....

"Um," he said when he called everywhere, "um."

"I wonder what I've done," I thought to myself. "I don't believe he likes my chest."

Without a word he got out his stethoscope and began to listen to me. As luck would have it, he struck something interesting almost at once, and for what seemed hours he stood there listening and listening to it. But it was boring for me, because I really had very little to do. I could have bitten him in the neck with some ease ... or I might have licked his ear. Beyond that, nothing seemed to offer.

I moistened my lips and spoke.

"Am I dying?" I asked in a broken voice.

"Don't talk," he said. "Just breathe naturally."

"I am dying," I thought, "and he is hiding it from me." It was a terrible reflection.

"Um," he said, and moved on.

By-and-by he went and listened behind my back. It is very bad form to listen behind a person's back. I did not tell him so however. I wanted him to like me.

"Yes," he said. "Now cough."

"I haven't a cough," I pointed out.

"Make the noise of coughing," he said severely.

Extremely nervous, I did my celebrated imitation of a man with an irritating cough.

"H'm! h'm! h'm! h'm!"

"Yes," said the doctor. "Go on."

"He likes it," I said to myself, "and he must obviously be an excellent judge. I shall devote more time to mimicry in future. H'm! h'm! h'm!..."

The doctor came round to where I could see him again.

"Now cough like this," he said. "Honk! Honk!"

I gave my celebrated imitation of a sick rhinoceros gasping out its life. It went well. I got an encore.

"Um," he said gravely, "um." He put his stethoscope away and looked earnestly at me.

"Tell me the worst," I begged. "I'm not bothering about this stupid insurance business now. That's off, of course. But—how long have I? I must put my affairs in order. Can you promise me a week?"

He said nothing. He took my wrists in his hands and pressed them. It was evident that grief over-mastered him and that he was taking a silent farewell of me. I bowed my head. Then, determined to bear my death-sentence like a man, I said firmly, "So be it," and drew myself away from him.

However, he wouldn't let me go.

"Come, come," I said to him, "you must not give way," and I made an effort to release one of my hands meaning to pat him encouragingly on the shoulder.

He resisted....

I realised suddenly that I had mistaken his meaning, and that he was simply feeling my pulses.

"Um," he said, "um," and continued to finger my wrists.

Clenching my teeth, and with the veins staring out on my forehead, I worked my pulses as hard as I could.

"Ah," he said, as I finished tying my tie; and he got up from the desk where he had been making notes of my disastrous case, and came over to me. "There is just one thing more. Sit down."

I sat down.

"Now cross your knees."

I crossed my knees. He bent over me and gave me a sharp tap below the knee with the side of his hand.

My chest may have disappointed him.... He may have disliked my back.... Possibly I was a complete failure with my pulses.... But I knew the knee-trick.

This time he should not be disappointed.

I was taking no risks. Almost before his hand reached my knee, my foot shot out and took him fairly under the chin. His face suddenly disappeared.

"I haven't got *that* disease," I said cheerily.

XXXIV. GETTING THE NEEDLE

He was a pale, enthusiastic young man of the name of Simms; and he held forth to us at great length about his latest hobby.

"Now I'll just show you a little experiment," he wound up, "one that I have never known to fail. First of all I want you to hide a needle somewhere, while I am out of the room. You must stick it where it can be seen—on a chair—or on the floor if you like. Then I shall come back blindfolded and find it."

"Oh, Mr. Simms!" we all said.

"Now, which one of you has the strongest will?"

We pushed Jack forward. Jack is at any rate a big man.

"Very well. I shall want you to take my hand when I come in, and look steadily at the needle—concentrate all your thoughts on it. I, on the other hand, shall make my mind a perfect blank. Then your thoughts will graduallypass into my brain, and I shall feel myself as it were, dragged in the direction of the needle."

"And I shall feel myself, as it were, dragged after you?" said Jack.

"Yes; you mustn't put any strain on my arm at all. Let me go just where I like, only *will* me to go in the right direction. Now then."

He took out his handkerchief, put it hastily back, and said: "First I shall want to borrow a handkerchief or something."

Well, we blindfolded him, and led him out of the room. Then Muriel got a needle, which, after some discussion, was stuck into the back of the Chesterfield. Simms returned and took Jack's left hand.

They stood there together, Jack frowning earnestly at the needle, and Simms swaying uncertainly at the knees. Suddenly his knees went in altogether, and he made a little zig-zag dash across the room, as though he were taking cover. Jack lumbered after him, instinctively bending his head, too. They were brought up by the piano, which Simms struck with great force. We all laughed, and Jack apologised.

"You told me to let you go where you liked, you know," he said.

"Yes, yes," said Simms rather peevishly, "but you should have willed me not to hit the piano."

As he spoke he tripped over a small stool and, flinging out an arm to save himself, swept two photograph frames off an occasional table.

"By Jove," said Jack, "that's jolly good. I saw you were going to do that, and I willed that the flower vase should be spared. I'm getting on."

"I think you had better start from the door again," I suggested. "Then you can get a clear run."

They took up their original positions.

"You must think hard, please," said Simms again. "My mind is a perfect blank, and yet I can feel nothing coming."

Jack made terrible faces at the needle. Then, without warning, Simms flopped on to the floor at full length, pulling Jack after him.

"You mustn't mind if I do that," he said, getting up slowly.

"No," said Jack, dusting himself.

"I felt irresistibly compelled to go down," said Simms.

"So did I," said Jack.

"The needle is very often hidden in the floor, you see. You are sure you are looking at it?"

They were in a corner with their back to it; and Jack, after trying in vain to get it over his right shoulder or his left, bent down and focussed it between his legs. This must have connected the current; for Simms turned right round and marched up to the needle.

"There!" he said triumphantly, taking off the bandage.

We all clapped, while Jack poured himself out a whisky. Simms turned to him.

"You have a very strong will indeed," he said, "one of the strongest I have met. Now, would one of the ladies like to try?"

"Oh, I'm sure I couldn't," said all the ladies.

"I should like to do it again," said Simms modestly. "Perhaps you, Sir?"

"All right, I'll try," I said.

When Simms was outside I told them my idea.

"I'll hold the needle in my other hand," I said, "and then I can always look at it easily, and it will always be in a different place, which ought to muddle him."

We fetched him in, and he took my left hand....

"No, it's no good," he said at last. "I don't seem to get it. Let me try the other hand."

I had no time to warn him. He clasped the other hand firmly; and from the shriek that followed it seemed that he got it. There ensued the "perfect blank" that he had insisted on all the evening. Then he pulled off the bandage, and showed a very angry face.

Well, we explained how accidental it was, and begged him to try again. He refused rather sulkily.

Suddenly Jack said: "I believe I could do it blindfolded. Miss Muriel, will you look at the needle, and see if you can will me?"

Simms bucked up a bit, and seemed keen on the idea. So Jack was blindfolded, the needle hid, and Muriel took his hand.

"Now is your mind a perfect blank?" said Simms to Jack.

"It always is," said Jack.

"Very well then. You ought soon to feel in a dreamy state, as though you were in another world. Miss Muriel, you must think only of the needle."

Jack held her hand tight, and looked most idiotically peaceful. After three minutes Simms spoke again.

"Well?" he said, eagerly.

"I've got the dreamy, other-world state perfectly," said Jack, and then he gave at the knees, just for the look of the thing.

"This is silly," said Muriel, trying to get her hand away.

Jack staggered violently, and gripped her hand again.

"Please, Miss Muriel," implored Simms. "I feel sure he is just going to do it."

Jack staggered again, sawed the air with his disengaged hand, and then turned right round and marched for the door, dragging Muriel behind him. The door slammed after them.

There is a little trick of sitting on a chair and picking a pin out of it with the teeth. I started Simms—who was all eagerness to follow the pair, and find out the mysterious force that was drawing them—upon this trick, for Jack is one of my best friends. When Jack and Muriel came back from the billiard-room and announced that they were engaged, Simms was on his back on the floor with the chair on the top of him—explaining, for the fourth time, that if the thing had not overbalanced at the critical moment he would have secured the object. There is much to be said for this view.

XXXV. DRESSING UP

"Then you really are coming?" said Queen Elizabeth.

"Yes, I really am," I sighed.

"What as?"

"I don't know at all—something with a cold. I leave it to you, partner, only don't go a black suit."

"What about Richelieu?"

"I should never be able to pronounce that," I confessed. "Besides, I always think that these great scientists—I should say philos—that is, of course, that these generals—er, which room is the Encyclopedia in?"

"You might go as one of the Kings of England. Which is your favourite King?"

"William and Mary. Now that would be an original costume. I should have——"

"Don't be ridiculous. Why not Henry VIII?"

"Do you think I should get a lot of partners as Henry VIII? Anyhow, I don't think it's a very becoming figure."

"But you don't wear fancy dress simply because it's becoming."

"Well, that is rather the point to settle. Are we going to enhance my natural beauty, or would you like it—er—toned down a little? Of course, I could go as the dog-faced man, only——"

"Very well then, if you don't like Henry, what about Edward I?"

"But why do you want to thrust royalty on me? I'd much sooner go as Perkin Warbeck. I should wear a brown perkin—I mean jerkin."

"Jack is going as Sir Walter Raleigh."

"Then I shall certainly touch him for a cigarette," I said, as I got up to go.

It was a week later that I met Elizabeth in Regent Street.

"Well," she said, "have you got your things?"

"I haven't," I confessed.

"I forgot who you said you were going as?"

"Somebody who had black hair," I said. "I have been thinking it over and I have come to the conclusion that I should have knocked them rather if I had had black hair. Instead of curly eyes and blue hair. Can you think of anybody for me?"

Queen Elizabeth regarded me as sternly as she might have regarded—Well, I'm not very good at history.

"Do you mean to say," she said at last, "that that is as far as you have got? Somebody who had black hair?"

"Hang it," I protested, "it's something to have been measured for the wig."

"Have you been measured for your wig?"

"Well—er—no. That is to say, not exactly what you might call measured. But—well, the fact is that I was just going along now, only—I say, where do I get a wig?"

"You've done nothing," said Elizabeth, "absolutely nothing."

"I say, don't say that," I began nervously, "I've done an awful lot, really. I've practically got the costume, I'm going as Harold the Boy Earl, or Jessica's last—Hallo, there's my bus; I've got a cold, I mustn't keep it waiting. Good-bye." And I fled.

"I am going," I said, "as Julius Cæsar. He was practically bald. Think how cool that will be."

"Do you mean to say," cried Elizabeth, "that you have altered again?"

"Don't be rough with me or I shall cry. I've got an awful cold."

"Then you've no business to go as Julius Cæsar."

"I say, now you're trying to unsettle me. And I was going to-morrow to order the clothes."

"What! You haven't——"

"I was really going this afternoon, only—only it's early closing day. Besides, I wanted to see if my cold would get better. Because if it didn't—— Look here, I'll be frank with you. I am going as Charlemagne."

"Oh!"

"Charlemagne in half-mourning, because Pepin the Short had just died. Something quiet in grey, with a stripe I thought. Only half-mourning because he only got half the throne. By-the-way, I suppose all these people wore pumps and white kid gloves all right? Yes, I thought so. I wonder if Charlemagne really had black hair. Anyhow, they can't prove he didn't, seeing when he lived. He flourished about 770, you know. As a matter of fact 770 wasn't actually his most flourishing year because the Radicals were in power then and land went down so. Now 771—Yes. Or else as Winston Churchill.

"Anyhow," I added indignantly a minute later, "I swear I'm going somehow."

"Hallo," I said cheerfully, as I ran into Her Majesty in Piccadilly, "I've just been ordering—that is to say, I've been going—I mean I'm just going to—— Let's see, it's next week, isn't it?"

For a moment Elizabeth was speechless—not at all my idea of the character.

"Now then," she said at last, "I am going to take you in hand. Will you trust yourself entirely to me?"

"To the death, Your Majesty. I'm sickening for something as it is."

"How tall are you?"

"Oh, more than that," I said quickly. "Gents' large medium, I am."

"Then I'll order a costume for you and have it sent round. There's no need for you to be anything historical; you might be a butcher."

"Quite—blue is my colour. In fact, I can do you the best end of the neck at tenpence, madam, if you'll wait a moment while I sharpen the knife. Let's see; you like it cut on the cross, I think? Bother, they've forgotten the strop."

"Well, it may not be a butcher," said Elizabeth; "it depends what they've got."

That was a week ago. This morning I was really ill at last; had hardly any breakfast; simply couldn't look a poached in the yolk. A day on the sofa in a darkened room and bed at seven o'clock was my programme. And then my eye caught a great box of clothes, and I remembered that the dance was to-night. I opened the box. Perhaps dressed soberly as a black-haired butcher I could look in for an hour or two ... and——

Help!

A yellow waistcoat, pink breeches, and—no, it's not an eider-down, it's a coat.

A yellow—Pink br——

I am going as Joseph.

I am going as a humming bird.

I am going—yes, that's it, I am going back to bed.

XXXVI. THE COMPLETE KITCHEN

I sat in the drawing-room after dinner with my knees together and my hands in my lap, and waited for the game to be explained to me.

"There's a pencil for you," said somebody.

"Thank you very much," I said and put it carefully away. Evidently I had won a forfeit already. It wasn't a very good pencil, though.

"Now, has everybody got pencils?" asked somebody else. "The game is called 'Furnishing a Kitchen.' It's quite easy. Will somebody think of a letter?" She turned to me. "Perhaps *you'd* better."

"Certainly," I said, and I immediately thought very hard of N. These thought-reading games are called different things, but they are all the same, really, and I don't believe in any of them.

"Well?" said everybody.

"What?... Yes, I have. Go on.... Oh, I beg your pardon," I said in confusion. "I thought you—N is the letter."

"N or M?"

I smiled knowingly to myself.

"My godfather and my godmother," I went on cautiously——

"It was N," interrupted somebody. "Now then, you've got five minutes in which to write down everything you can beginning with N. Go." And they all started to write like anything.

I took my pencil out and began to think. I know it sounds an easy game to you now, as you sit at your desk surrounded by dictionaries;

but when you are squeezed on to the edge of a sofa, given a very blunt pencil and a thin piece of paper, and challenged to write in five minutes (on your knees) all the words you can think of beginning with a certain letter—well, it is another matter altogether. I thought of no end of things which started with K, or even L; I thought of "rhinoceros" which is a very long word and starts with R; but as for——

I looked at my watch and groaned. One minute gone.

"I must keep calm," I said and in a bold hand I wrote *Napoleon.* Then after a moment's thought, I added *Nitro-glycerine*, and *Nats.*

"This is splendid," I told myself. "*Nottingham, Nobody and Noon.* That makes six."

At six I stuck for two minutes. I did worse than that in fact; for I suddenly remembered that gnats were spelt with a G. However, I decided to leave them, in case nobody else remembered. And on the fourth minute I added *Non-sequitur.*

"Time!" said somebody.

"Just a moment," said everybody. They wrote down another word or two (which isn't fair), and then began to add up. "I've got thirty," said one.

"Thirty-two."

"Twenty-five."

"Good Heavens," I said, "I've only got seven."

There was a shout of laughter.

209

"Then you'd better begin," said somebody. "Read them out."

I coughed nervously, and began.

"Napoleon."

There was another shout of laughter.

"I am afraid we can't allow that."

"Why ever not?" I asked in amazement.

"Well, you'd hardly find him in a kitchen, would you?"

I took out a handkerchief and wiped my brow. "I don't want to find him in a kitchen," I said nervously. "Why should I? As a matter of fact he's dead. I don't see what the kitchen's got to do with it. Kitchens begin with a K."

"But the game is called 'Furnishing a Kitchen.' You have to make a list of things beginning with N which you would find in a kitchen. You understood that, didn't you?"

"Y-y-yes," I said. "Oh, y-y-y-yes. Of course."

"So Napoleon——"

I pulled myself together with a great effort.

"You don't understand," I said with dignity. "The cook's name was Napoleon."

"Cooks aren't called Napoleon," said everybody.

"This one was. Carrie Napoleon. Her mistress was just as surprised at first as you were, but Carrie assured her that——"

"No, I'm afraid we can't allow it."

"I'm sorry," I said; "I'm wrong about that. Her name was Carrie Smith. But her young man was a soldier, and she had bought a Life of Napoleon for a birthday present for him. It stood on the dresser waiting for her next Sunday out."

"Oh! Oh, well, I suppose that is possible. Go on."

"Gnats," I went on nervously and hastily. "Of course I know that——"

"Gnats are spelt with a G," they shrieked.

"These weren't. They had lost the G when they were quite young, and consequently couldn't bite at all, and Cook said that——"

"No; I'm afraid not."

"I'm sorry," I said resignedly. "I had about forty of them—on the dresser. If you won't allow any of them, it pulls me down a lot. Er—then we have Nitro-glycerine."

There was another howl of derision.

"Not at all," I said haughtily. "Cook had chapped hands very badly, and she went to the chemist's one evening for a little glycerine. The chemist was out, and his assistant—a very nervous young fellow—gave her nitro-glycerine by mistake. It stood on the dresser, it did, really."

"Well," said everybody very reluctantly, "I suppose——"

I went on hastily.

"That's two. Then Nobody. Of course, you might easily find nobody in the kitchen. In fact you would pretty often, I should say. Three. The next is Noon. It could be noon in the kitchen as well as anywhere else. Don't be narrow-minded about that."

"All right. Go on."

"Non-sequitur," I said doubtfully.

"What on earth——"

"It's a little difficult to explain, but the idea is this. At most restaurants you can get a second help of anything for half-price, and that is technically called a 'follow.' Now, if they didn't give you a follow, that would be a Non-sequitur.... You do see that, don't you?"

There was a deadly silence.

"Five," I said cheerfully. "The last is Nottingham. I must confess," I added magnanimously, "that I am a bit doubtful whether you would actually find Nottingham in a kitchen."

"You don't say so!"

"Yes. My feeling is that you would be more likely to find the kitchen in Nottingham. On the other hand, it is just possible that as Calais was found engraven on Mary's heart, so—Oh, very well. Then it remains at five."

Of course you think that as I only had five, I came out last. But you are wrong. There is a pleasing rule in this game that, if you have any word in your list which somebody else has, you cannot count it. And as all the others had the obvious things—such as a nutmeg-grater or a neck of mutton, or a nomlette—my five won easily. And you will note that if only I had been allowed to count my gnats, it would have been forty-five.

XXXVII. AN INFORMAL EVENING

Dinner was a very quiet affair. Not a soul drew my chair away from under me as I sat down, and during the meal nobody threw bread about. We talked gently of art and politics and things; and when the ladies left there was no booby trap waiting for them at the door. In a word, nothing to prepare me for what was to follow.

We strolled leisurely into the drawing-room. A glance told me the worst. The ladies were in a cluster round Miss Power, and Miss Power was on the floor. She got up quickly as we came in.

"We were trying to go underneath the poker," she explained. "Can you do it?"

I waved the poker back.

"Let me see you do it again," I said. "I missed the first part."

"Oh, I can never do it. Bob, you show us."

Bob is an active young fellow. He took the poker, rested the end on the floor, and then twisted himself underneath his right arm. I expected to see him come up inside out, but he looked much the same after it. However, no doubt his organs are all on the wrong side now.

"Yes, that's how I should do it," I said hastily.

But Miss Power was firm. She gave me the poker. I pressed it hard on the floor, said good-bye to them all, and dived. I got half-way round, and was supporting myself upside down by one toe and the slippery end of the poker, when it suddenly occurred to me that the earth was revolving at an incredible speed on its own axis, and that, in addition, we were hurtling at thousands of miles a minute round the sun. It seemed impossible in these circumstances that I should keep my balance any longer; and as soon as I realised this the poker began to slip. I was in no sort of position to do anything about it, and we came down heavily together.

"Oh, what a pity!" said Miss Power. "I quite thought you'd done it."

"Being actually on the spot," I said, "I knew that I hadn't."

"Do try again."

"Not till the ground's a little softer."

"Let's do the jam-pot trick," said another girl.

"I'm not going under a jam-pot for anybody," I murmured.

However, it turned out that this trick was quite different. You place a book (Macaulay's *Essays* or what not) on the jam-pot and sit on the book, one heel only touching the ground. In the right hand you have a box of matches, in the left a candle. The jam-pot, of course, is on its side, so that it can roll beneath you. Then you light the candle ... and hand it to anybody who wants to go to bed.

I was ready to give way to the ladies here, but even while I was bowing and saying, "Not at all," I found myself on one of the jam-pots with Bob next to me on another. To balance with the arms outstretched was not so difficult; but as the matches were then about six feet from the candle and there seemed no way of getting them nearer together the solution of the problem was as remote as ever. Three times I brought my hands together, and three times the jam-pot left me.

"Well played, Bob," said somebody. The bounder has done it.

I looked at his jam-pot.

"There you are," I said. "'Raspberry—1909.' Mine's 'Gooseberry—1911,' a rotten vintage. And look at my book, *Alone on the Prairie*; and you've got *The Mormon's Wedding*. No wonder I couldn't do it."

I refused to try it again as I didn't think I was being treated fairly; and after Bob and Miss Power had had a race at it, which Bob won, we got on to something else.

"Of course you can pick a pin out of a chair with your teeth?" said Miss Power.

"Not properly," I said. "I always swallow the pin."

"I suppose it doesn't count if you swallow the pin," said Miss Power thoughtfully.

"I don't know. I've never really thought about that side of it much. Anyhow, unless you've got a whole lot of pins you don't want, don't ask me to do it to-night."

Accordingly we passed on to the water-trick. I refused at this, but Miss Power went full length on the floor with a glass of water balanced on her forehead and came up again without spilling a single drop. Personally I shouldn't have minded spilling a single drop; it was the thought of spilling the whole glass that kept me back. Anyway it is a useless trick, the need for which never arises in an ordinary career. Picking up *The Times* with the teeth, while clasping the left ankle with the right hand, is another matter. That might come in useful on occasions; as, for instance, if, having lost your left arm on the field and having to staunch with the right hand the flow of blood from a bullet wound in the opposite ankle, you desired to glance through the Financial Supplement while waiting for the ambulance.

"Here's a nice little trick," broke in Bob, as I was preparing myself in this way for the German invasion.

He had put two chairs together, front to front, and was standing over them, if that conveys it to you. Then he jumped up, turned round in the air, and came down facing the other way.

"Can *you* do it?" I said to Miss Power.

"Come and try," said Bob to me. "It's not really difficult."

I went and stood over the chairs. Then I moved them apart and walked over to my hostess.

"Good-bye," I said; "I'm afraid I must go now."

"Coward!" said somebody, who knew me rather better than the others.

"It's much easier than you think," said Bob.

"I don't think it's easy at all," I protested. "I think it's impossible."

I went back and stood over the chairs again. For some time I waited there in deep thought. Then I bent my knees preparatory to the spring, straightened them up, and said,

"What happens if you just miss it?"

"I suppose you bark your shins a bit."

"Yes, that's what I thought."

I bent my knees again, worked my arms up and down, and then stopped suddenly and said:

"What happens if you miss it pretty easily?"

"Oh, *you* can do it, if Bob can," said Miss Power kindly.

"He's practised. I expect he started with two hassocks and worked up to this. I'm not afraid, but I want to know the possibilities. If it's only a broken leg or two, I don't mind. If it's permanent disfigurement I think I ought to consult my family first."

I jumped up and came down again the same way for practice.

"Very well," I said. "Now I'm going to try. I haven't the faintest hope of doing it, but you all seem to want to see an accident, and anyhow, I'm not going to be called a coward. One, two, three...."

"Well done," cried everybody.

"Did I do it?" I whispered, as I sat on the floor and pressed a cushion against my shins.

"Rather!"

"Then," I said, massaging my ankles, "next time I shall try to miss."

XXXVIII. A BILLIARD LESSON

I was showing Celia a few fancy strokes on the billiard table. The other members of the house-party were in the library, learning their parts for some approaching theatricals—that is to say, they were sitting round the fire and saying to each other, "This *is* a rotten play." We had been offered the position of auditors to several of the company, but we were going to see *Parsifal* on the next day, and I was afraid that the constant excitement would be bad for Celia.

"Why don't you ask me to play with you?" she asked. "You never teach me anything."

"There's ingratitude. Why, I gave you your first lesson at golf only last Thursday."

"So you did. I know golf. Now show me billiards."

I looked at my watch.

"We've only twenty minutes. I'll play you thirty up."

"Right-o. What do you give me—a ball or a bisque or what?"

"I can't spare you a ball, I'm afraid. I shall want all three when I get going. You may have fifteen start, and I'll tell you what to do."

"Well, what do I do first?"

"Select a cue."

She went over to the rack and inspected them.

"This seems a nice brown one. Now then, you begin."

"Celia, you've got the half-butt. Put it back and take a younger one."

"I thought it seemed taller than the others." She took another. "How's this? Good. Then off you go."

"Will you be spot or plain?" I said, chalking my cue.

"Does it matter?"

"Not very much. They're both the same shape."

"Then what's the difference?"

"Well, one is more spotted than the other."

"Then I'll be less spotted."

I went to the table.

"I think," I said, "I'll try and screw in off the red." (I did this once by accident and I've always wanted to do it again.) "Or perhaps," I corrected myself, as soon as the ball had left me, "I had better give a safety miss."

I did. My ball avoided the red and came swiftly back into the left-hand bottom pocket.

"That's three to you," I said without enthusiasm.

Celia seemed surprised.

"But I haven't begun yet," she said. "Well, I suppose you know the rules, but it seems funny. What would you like me to do?"

"Well, there isn't much on. You'd better just try and hit the red ball."

"Right." She leant over the table and took long and careful aim. I held my breath.... Still she aimed.... Then keeping her chin on the cue, she slowly turned her head and looked up at me with a thoughtful expression.

"Oughtn't there to be three balls on the table?" she said, wrinkling her forehead.

"No," I answered shortly.

"But why not?"

"Because I went down by mistake."

"But you said that when you got going, you wanted—— I can't argue bending down like this." She raised herself slowly. "You said——Oh, all right, I expect you know. Anyhow, I have scored some already, haven't I?"

"Yes. You're eighteen to my nothing."

"Yes. Well, now I shall have to aim all over again." She bent slowly over her cue. "Does it matter where I hit the red?"

"Not much. As long as you hit it on the red part."

She hit it hard on the side, and both balls came into baulk.

"Too good," I said.

"Does either of us get anything for it?"

"No." The red and white were close together, and I went up the table and down again, on the off-chance of a cannon. I misjudged it, however.

"That's three to you," I said stiffly, as I took my ball out of the right-hand bottom pocket. "Twenty-one to nothing."

"Funny how I'm doing all the scoring," said Celia meditatively. "And I've practically never played before. I shall hit the red hard now and see what happens to it."

She hit, and the red coursed madly about the table, coming to rest near the top right-hand pocket and close to the cushion. With a forcing shot I could get in.

"This will want a lot of chalk," I said pleasantly to Celia, and gave it plenty. Then I let fly....

"Why did that want a lot of chalk?" said Celia with interest.

I went to the fireplace and picked my ball out of the fender.

"That's three to you," I said coldly. "Twenty-four to nothing."

"Am I winning?"

"You're leading," I explained. "Only, you see, I may make a twenty at any moment."

"Oh!" She thought this over. "Well, I may make my three at any moment."

She chalked her cue and went over to her ball.

"What shall I do?"

"Just touch the red on the right-hand side," I said, "and you'll go into the pocket."

"The right-hand side? Do you mean my right-hand side or the ball's?"

"The right-hand side of the ball, of course; that is to say, the side opposite your right-hand."

"But its right-hand side is opposite my left hand, if the ball is facing this way."

"Take it," I said wearily, "that the ball has its back to you."

"How rude of it," said Celia, and hit it on the left-hand side, and sank it. "Was that what you meant?"

"Well ... it's another way of doing it."

"I thought it was. What do I give you for that?"

"You get three."

"Oh, I thought the other person always got the marks. I know the last three times——"

"Go on," I said freezingly. "You have another turn."

"Oh, is it like rounders?"

"Something. Go on, there's a dear. It's getting late."

She went, and left the red over the middle pocket.

"A-ha!" I said. I found a nice place in the "D" for my ball. "Now then. This is the Grey stroke, you know."

I suppose I was nervous. Anyhow, I just nicked the red ball gently on the wrong side and left it hanging over the pocket. The white travelled slowly up the table.

"Why is that called the Grey stroke?" asked Celia with great interest.

"Because once, when Sir Edward Grey was playing the German Ambassador—but it's rather a long story. I'll tell you another time."

"Oh! Well, anyhow, did the German Ambassador get anything for it?"

"No."

"Then I suppose I don't. Bother." "But you've only got to knock the red in for game."

"Oh!... There, what's that?"

"That's a miscue. I get one."

"Oh!... Oh, well," she added magnanimously, "I'm glad you've started scoring. It will make it more interesting for you."

There was just room to creep in off the red, leaving it still over the pocket. With Celia's ball nicely over the other pocket there was a chance of my twenty break. "Let's see," I said, "how many do I want?"

"Twenty-nine," replied Celia.

"Ah," I said ... and I crept in.

"That's three to you," I said icily. "Game."

XXXIX. BACHELOR RELICS

"Do you happen to want," I said to Henry, "an opera hat that doesn't op? At least it only works one side."

"No," said Henry.

"To any one who buys my opera hat for a large sum I am giving away four square yards of linoleum, a revolving bookcase, two curtain rods, a pair of spring-grip dumb-bells and an extremely patent mouse-trap."

"No," said Henry again.

"The mouse-trap," I pleaded, "is unused. That is to say, no mouse has used it yet. My mouse-trap has never been blooded."

"I don't want it myself," said Henry, "but I know a man who does."

"Henry, you know everybody. For Heaven's sake introduce me to your friend. Why does he particularly want a mouse-trap?"

"He doesn't. He wants anything that's old. Old clothes, old carpets, anything that's old he'll buy."

He seemed to be exactly the man I wanted.

"Introduce me to your fellow clubman," I said firmly.

That evening I wrote to Henry's friend, Mr. Bennett. "Dear Sir," I wrote, "if you would call upon me to-morrow I should like to show you some really old things, all genuine antiques. In particular I would call your attention to an old opera hat of exquisite workmanship, and a mouse-trap of chaste and handsome design. I have also a few yards of Queen Anne linoleum of a circular pattern which I think will please you. My James the First spring-grip dumb-bells and Louis Quatorze curtain-rods are well known to connoisseurs. A genuine old cork bedroom suite, comprising one bath-mat, will also be included in the sale. Yours faithfully."

On second thoughts I tore the letter up and sent Mr. Bennett a postcard asking him to favour the undersigned with a call at 10.30 prompt. And at 10.30 prompt he came.

I had expected to see a bearded patriarch with a hooked nose and three hats on his head, but Mr. Bennett turned out to be a very spruce gentleman, wearing (I was sorry to see) much better clothes than the opera hat I proposed to sell him. He became businesslike at once.

"Just tell me what you want to sell," he said, whipping out a pocket-book, "and I'll make a note of it. I take anything."

I looked round my spacious apartment and wondered what to begin with.

"The revolving bookcase," I announced.

"I'm afraid there's very little sale for revolving bookcases now," he said, as he made a note of it.

"As a matter of fact," I pointed out, "this one doesn't revolve. It got stuck some years ago."

He didn't seem to think that this would increase the rush, but he made a note of it.

"Then the writing-desk."

"The what?"

"The Georgian bureau. A copy of an old twentieth-century escritoire."

"Walnut?" he said, tapping it.

"Possibly. The value of this Georgian writing-desk, however, lies not in the wood but in the literary associations."

"Ah! My customers don't bother much about that, but still—whose was it?"

"Mine!" I said with dignity, placing my hand in the breast pocket of my coat. "I have written many charming things at that desk. My 'Ode to a Bell-push,' my 'Thoughts on Asia,' my——"

"Anything else in this room?" said Mr. Bennett. "Carpets, curtains——"

"Nothing else," I said coldly.

We went into the bedroom and, gazing on the linoleum, my enthusiasm returned to me.

"The linoleum," I said, with a wave of the hand.

"Very much worn," said Mr. Bennett.

I called his attention to the piece under the bed.

"Not under there," I said. "I never walk on that piece. It's as good as new."

He made a note. "What else?" he said.

I showed him round the collection. He saw the Louis Quatorze curtain-rods, the cork bedroom suite, the Cæsarian nail-brush (quite bald), the antique shaving-mirror with genuine crack—he saw it all. And then we went back into the other rooms and found some more things for him.

"Yes," he said, consulting his notebook. "And now how would you like me to buy these?"

"At a large price," I said. "If you have brought your cheque-book I'll lend you a pen."

"You want me to make you an offer? Otherwise I should sell them by auction for you, deducting ten per cent. commission."

"Not by auction," I said impulsively. "I couldn't bear to know how much or rather how little, my Georgian bureau fetched. It was there, as I think I told you, that I wrote my 'Guide to the Round Pond.' Give me an inclusive price for the lot, and never, never let me know the details."

He named an inclusive price. It was something under a hundred-and-fifty pounds. I shouldn't have minded that if it had only been a little over ten pounds. But it wasn't.

"Right," I agreed. "And, oh, I was nearly forgetting. There's an old opera hat of exquisite workmanship, which——"

"Ah, now clothes had much better be sold by auction. Make a pile of all you don't want and I'll send round a sack for them: I have an auction sale every Wednesday."

"Very well. Send round to-morrow. And you might—er—also send round a—er—cheque for—quite so. Well, then good morning."

When he had gone I went into my bedroom and made a pile of my opera-hat. It didn't look very impressive—hardly worth having a sack specially sent round for it. To keep it company I collected an assortment of clothes. It pained me to break up my wardrobe in this way, but I wanted the bidding for my opera-hat to be brisk, and a few preliminary suits would warm the public up. Altogether it was a goodly pile when it was done. The opera-hat perched on the top, half of it only at work.

To-day I received from Mr. Bennett a cheque, a catalogue and an account. The catalogue was marked "Lots 172-179." Somehow I felt that my opera hat would be Lot 176. I turned to it in the account.

"*Lot 176—Six shillings*"

"It did well," I said. "Perhaps in my heart of hearts I hoped for seven and sixpence, but six shillings—yes, it was a good hat."

And then I turned to the catalogue.

"*Lot 176*—Frock coat and vest, dress coat and vest, ditto, pair of trousers and opera hat."

"*And opera hat.*" Well, well. At least it had the position of honour at the end. My opera hat was starred.

LITTLE PLAYS FOR AMATEURS

[Note.—*There are only six plots allowed to us who are not professionals. Here they are. When you have read them, then you will know all about amateur theatricals.*]

XL. "FAIR MISTRESS DOROTHY"

The scene is an apartment in the mansion of Sir Thomas Farthingale. *There is no need to describe the furniture in it, as rehearsals will gradually show what is wanted. A picture or two of previous* Sir Thomas's *might be seen on the walls, if you have an artistic friend who could arrange this; but it is a mistake to hang up your own ancestors, as some of your guests may recognise them, and thus pierce beneath the vraisemblance of the scene.*

The period is that of Cromwell—sixteen something.

The costumes are, as far as possible, of the same period.

Mistress Dorothy Farthingale *is seated in the middle of the stage, reading a letter and occasionally sighing.*

Enter My Lord Carey.

Carey. Mistress Dorothy alone! Truly Fortune smiles upon me.

Dorothy (*hiding the letter quickly*). An she smiles, my lord, I needs must frown.

Carey (*used to this sort of thing and no longer put off by it*). Nay, give me but one smile, sweet mistress. (*She sighs heavily.*) You sigh! Is't for me?

Dorothy (*feeling that the sooner he and the audience understand the situation the better*). I sigh for another, my lord, who is absent.

Carey (*annoyed*). Zounds, and zounds again! A pest upon the fellow! (*He strides up and down the room, keeping out of the way of his sword as much as possible.*) Would that I might pink the pesky knave!

Dorothy (*turning upon him a look of hate*). Would that you might have the chance, my lord, so it were in fair fighting. Methinks Roger's sword-arm will not have lost its cunning in the wars.

Carey. A traitor to fight against his King.

Dorothy. He fights for what he thinks is right. (*She takes out his letter and kisses it.*)

Carey (*observing the action*). You have a letter from him!

Dorothy (*hastily concealing it and turning pale*). How know you that?

Carey. Give it to me! (*She shrieks and rises.*) By heavens, madam, I will have it! (*He struggles with her and seizes it.*)

Enter Sir Thomas.

Sir Thomas. Odds life, my lord, what means this?

Carey (*straightening himself*). It means, Sir Thomas, that you harbour a rebel within your walls. Master Roger Dale, traitor, corresponds secretly with your daughter.

(*Who, I forgot to say, has swooned.*)

Sir Thomas (*sternly*). Give me the letter. Ay, 'tis Roger's hand, I know it well. (*He reads the letter, which is full of thoughtful metaphors about love, aloud to the audience. Suddenly his eyebrows go up and down to express surprise. He seizes* Lord Carey *by the arm.*) Ha! Listen! "To-morrow when the sun is upon the western window of the gallery, I will be with thee." The villain!

Carey (*who does not know the house very well*). When is that?

Sir Thomas. Why, 'tis now, for I have but recently passed through the gallery and did mark the sun.

Carey (*fiercely*). In the name of the King, Sir Thomas, I call upon you to arrest this traitor.

Sir Thomas (*sighing*). I loved the boy well, yet——

(*He shrugs his shoulders expressively and goes out with* Lord Carey *to collect sufficient force for the arrest.*)

Enter Roger *by secret door R.*

Roger. My love!

Dorothy (*opening her eyes*). Roger!

Roger. At last!

(*For the moment they talk in short sentences like this. Then* Dorothy *puts her hand to her brow as if she is remembering something horrible.*)

Dorothy. Roger! Now I remember! It is not safe for you to stay!

Roger (*very brave*). Am I a puling child to be afraid?

Dorothy. My Lord Carey is here. He has read your letter.

Roger. The black-livered dog! Would I had him at my sword's point to teach him manners.

(*He puts his hand to his heart and staggers into a chair.*)

Dorothy. Oh, you are wounded!

Roger. Faugh, 'tis but a scratch. Am I a puling——

(*He faints. She binds up his ankle.*)

Enter Lord Carey *with two soldiers.*

Carey. Arrest this traitor! (*Roger is led away by the soldiers.*)

Dorothy (*stretching out her hands to him*). Roger! (*She sinks into a chair.*)

Carey (*choosing quite the wrong moment for a proposal*). Dorothy, I love you! Think no more of this traitor, for he will surely hang. 'Tis your father's wish that you and I should wed.

Dorothy (*refusing him*). Go, lest I call in the grooms to whip you.

Carey. By heaven—— (*Thinking better of it.*) I go to fetch your father.

(*Exit.*)

Enter Roger *by secret door L.*

Dorothy. Roger! You have escaped.

Roger. Knowest not the secret passage from the wine cellar, where we so often played as children? 'Twas in that same cellar the thick-skulled knaves immured me.

Dorothy. Roger, you must fly! Wilt wear a cloak of mine to elude our enemies?

Roger (*missing the point rather*). Nay, if I die, let me die like a man, not like a puling girl. Yet, sweetheart——

Enter Lord Carey *by ordinary door.*

Carey (*forgetting himself in his confusion*). Odds my zounds, dod sink me! What murrain is this?

Roger (*seizing Sir Thomas's sword, which had been accidentally left behind on the table, as I ought to have said before, and advancing threateningly*). It means, my lord, that a villain's time has come. Wilt say a prayer?

(*They fight, and Carey is disarmed before they can hurt each other.*)

Carey (*dying game*). Strike, Master Dale!

Roger. Nay, I cannot kill in cold blood.

(*He throws down his sword. Lord Carey exhibits considerable emotion at this, and decides to turn over an entirely new leaf.*)

Enter two soldiers.

Carey. Arrest that man! (Roger *is seized again.*) Mistress Dorothy, it is for you to say what shall be done with the prisoner.

Dorothy (*standing up if she was sitting down, and sitting down if she was standing up*). Ah, give him to me, my lord!

Carey (*joining the hands of Roger and Dorothy*). I trust to you, sweet mistress, to see that the prisoner does not escape again.

(Dorothy *and* Roger *embrace each other, if they can do it without causing a scandal in the neighbourhood, and the curtain goes down.*)

XLI. "A SLIGHT MISUNDERSTANDING"

The scene is a drawing-room (in which the men are allowed to smoke—or a smoking-room in which the women are allowed to draw—it doesn't much matter) in the house of somebody or other in the country. George Turnbull *and his old College friend,* Henry Peterson, *are confiding in each other, as old friends will, over their whiskies and cigars. It is about three o'clock in the afternoon.*

George (*dreamily, helping himself to a stiff soda*). Henry, do you remember that evening at Christ Church College, five years ago, when we opened our hearts to each other?...

Henry (*lighting a cigar and hiding it in a fern-pot*). That moonlight evening on the Backs, George, when I had failed in my Matriculation examination?

George. Yes; and we promised that when either of us fell in love the other should be the first to hear of it? (*Rising solemnly.*) Henry, the moment has come. (*With shining eyes.*) I am in love.

Henry (*jumping up and grasping him by both hands*). George! My dear old George! (*In a voice broken with emotion.*) Bless you, George!

(*He pats him thoughtfully on the back three times, nods his own head twice, gives him a final grip of the hand, and returns to his chair.*)

George (*more moved by this than he cares to show*). Thank you, Henry. (*Hoarsely.*) You're a good fellow.

Henry (*airily, with a typically British desire to conceal his emotion*). Who is the lucky little lady?

George (*taking out a picture postcard of the British Museum and kissing it passionately*). Isobel Barley!

(*If Henry is not careful he will probably give a start of surprise here, with the idea of suggesting to the audience that he* (1) *knows something about the lady's past, or* (2) *is in love with her himself. He is, however, thinking of a different play. We shall come to that one in a moment.*)

Henry (*in a slightly dashing manner*). Little Isobel? Lucky dog!

George. I wish I could think so. (*Sighs.*) But I have yet to approach her, and she may be another's. (*Fiercely.*) Heavens, Henry, if she should be another's!

Enter Isobel.

Isobel (*brightly*). So I've run you to earth at last. Now what have you got to say for yourselves?

Henry (*like a man*). By Jove! (*Looking at his watch.*) I had no idea— is it really—poor old Joe—waiting——

(*Dashes out tactfully in a state of incoherence.*)

George (*rising and leading* Isobel *to the front of the stage*). Miss Barley, now that we are alone I have something I want to say to you.

Isobel (*looking at her watch*). Well, you must be quick. Because I'm engaged.

(*George drops her hand and staggers away from her.*)

Isobel. Why, what's the matter?

George (*to the audience, in a voice expressing the very deeps of emotion*). Engaged! She is engaged! I am too late!

(*He sinks into a chair, and covers his face with his hands.*)

Isobel (*surprised*). Mr. Turnbull! What has happened?

George (*waving her away with one hand*). Go! Leave me! I can bear this best alone. (*Exit Isobel.*) Merciful heavens, she is plighted to another.

Enter Henry.

Henry (*eagerly*). Well, old man?

George (*raising a face white with misery—that is to say, if he has remembered to put the French chalk in the palms of his hands*). Henry, I am too late! She is another's!

Henry (*in surprise*). Whose?

George (*with dignity*). I did not ask her. It is nothing to me. Good-bye, Henry. Be kind to her.

Henry. Why, where are you going?

George (*firmly*). To the Rocky Mountains. I shall shoot some bears. Grizzly ones. It may be that thus I shall forget my grief.

Henry (*after a pause*). Perhaps you are right, George. What shall I tell—her?

George. Tell her—nothing. But should anything (*feeling casually in his pockets*) happen to me—if (*going over them again quickly*) I do not come back, then (*searching them all, including the waist coat ones, in desperate haste*) give her, give her, give her (*triumphantly bringing his handkerchief out of the last pocket*) this, and say that my last thought was of her. Good-bye, my old friend. Good-bye.

(*Exit to Rocky Mountains.*)

Enter Isobel.

Isobel. Why, where's Mr. Turnbull?

Henry (*sadly*). He's gone.

Isobel. Gone? Where?

Henry. To the Rocky Mountains. To shoot bears. (*Feeling that some further explanation is needed.*) Grizzly ones.

Isobel. But he was *here* a moment ago.

Henry. Yes, he's only *just* gone.

Isobel. Why didn't he say good-bye? (*Eagerly.*) But perhaps he left a message for me? (*Henry shakes his head.*) Nothing? (*Henry bows silently and leaves the room.*) Oh! (*She gives a cry and throws herself on the sofa.*) And I loved him! George, George, why didn't you speak?

Enter George *hurriedly. He is fully dressed for a shooting expedition in the Rocky Mountains, and carries a rifle under his arm.*

George (*to the audience*). I have just come back for my pocket-handkerchief. I must have dropped it in here somewhere. (*He begins to search for it, and in the ordinary course of things comes upon Isobel on the sofa. He puts his rifle down carefully on a table, with the muzzle pointing at the prompter rather than at the audience, and staggers back.*) Merciful heavens! Isobel! Dead! (*He falls on his knees beside the sofa.*) My love, speak to me!

Isobel (*softly*). George!

George. She is alive! Isobel!

Isobel. Don't go, George!

George. My dear, I love you! But when I heard that you were another's, honour compelled me———

Isobel (*sitting up quickly*). What do you mean by another's?

George. You said you were engaged!

Isobel (*suddenly realising how the dreadful misunderstanding arose which nearly wrecked two lives*). But I only meant I was engaged to play tennis with Lady Carbrook!

George. What a fool I have been! (*He hurries on before the audience can assent.*) Then, Isobel, you *will* be mine?

Isobel. Yes, George. And you won't go and shoot nasty bears, will you, dear? Not even grizzly ones?

George (*taking her in his arms*). Never, darling. That was only (*turning to the audience with the air of one who is making his best point*) A slight misunderstanding.

CURTAIN.

XLII. "MISS PRENDERGAST"

As the curtain goes up two ladies are discovered in the morning-room of Honeysuckle Lodge engaged in work of a feminine nature. Miss Alice Prendergast *is doing something delicate with a crochet-hook, but it is obvious that her thoughts are far away. She sighs at intervals and occasionally lays down her work and presses both hands to her heart. A sympathetic audience will have no difficulty in guessing that she is in love. On the other hand, her elder sister,* Miss Prendergast, *is completely wrapped up in a sock for one of the poorer classes, over which she frowns formidably. The sock, however, has no real bearing upon the plot, and she must not make too much of it.*

Alice (*hiding her emotions*). Did you have a pleasant dinner-party last night, Jane?

Jane (*to herself*). Seventeen, eighteen, nineteen, twenty. (*Looking up.*) Very pleasant indeed, Alice. The Blizzards were there, and the Podbys, and the Slumphs. (*These people are not important and should not be over-emphasised.*) Mrs. Podby's maid has given notice.

Alice. Who took you in?

Jane (*brightening up*). Such an interesting man, my dear. He talked most agreeably about Art during dinner, and we renewed the conversation in the drawing-room. We found that we agreed upon all the main principles of Art, considered as such.

Alice (*with a look in her eyes which shows that she is recalling a tender memory*). When I was in Shropshire last week—— What was your man's name?

Jane (*with a warning glance at the audience*). You know how difficult it is to catch names when one is introduced. I am certain he never heard mine. (*As the plot depends partly upon this, she pauses for it to sink in.*) But I enquired about him afterwards, and I find that he is a Mr.——

Enter Mary, *the parlourmaid.*

Mary (handing letter). A letter for you, Miss.

Jane (*taking it*). Thank you, Mary. (*Exit* Mary *to work up her next line.*) A letter! I wonder who it is from! (*Reading the envelope.*) "Miss Prendergast, Honeysuckle Lodge." (*She opens it with the air of one who has often received letters before, but feels that this one may play an important part in her life.*) "Dear Miss Prendergast, I hope you will pardon the presumption of what I am about to write to you, but whether you pardon me or not, I ask you to listen to me. I know of no woman for whose talents I have a greater admiration or for whose qualities I have a more sincere affection than yourself. Since I have known you, you have been the lodestar of my existence, the fountain of my inspiration. I feel that, were your life joined to mine, the joint path upon which we trod would be the path to happiness, such as I have as yet hardly dared to dream of. In short, dear Miss Prendergast, I ask you to marry me, and I will come in person for my answer. Yours truly (*in a voice of intense surprise*) Jas. Bootle!"

(*At the word "Bootle" a wave of warm colour rushes over Alice and dyes her from neck to brow. If she is not an actress of sufficient calibre to ensure this, she must do the best she can by starting abruptly and putting her hand to her throat.*)

Alice (*aside, in a choking voice*). Mr. Bootle! In love with Jane!

Jane. My dear! The man who took me down to dinner! Well!

Alice (*picking up her work again and trying to be calm*). What will you say?

Jane (*rather pleased with herself*). Well, really—I—this is—Mr. Bootle! Fancy!

Alice (*starting up*). Was that a ring? (*She frowns at the prompter and a bell is heard to ring.*) It is Mr. Bootle! I know his ring, I mean I know—— Dear, I think I will go and lie down. I have a headache.

(*She looks miserably at the audience, closes her eyes, and goes off with her handkerchief to her mouth, taking care not to fall over the furniture.*)

Enter Mary, *followed by James Bootle.*

Mary. Mr. Bootle. (*Exit finally.*)

Jane. Good morning, Mr. Bootle.

Bootle. I beg—I thought—why, of course! It's Miss—er—h'm, yes. How do you do? Did you get back safely last night?

Jane. Yes, thank you. (*Coyly.*) I got your letter.

Bootle. My letter? (*Sees his letter on the table. Furiously.*) You opened my letter!

Jane (*mistaking his fury for passion*). Yes, James. And (*looking down on the ground*) the answer is "Yes."

Bootle (*realising the situation*). By George! (*Aside.*) I have proposed to the wrong lady. Tchck!

243

Jane. You may kiss me, James.

Bootle. Have you a sister?

Jane (*missing the connection*). Yes, I have a younger sister, Alice. (*Coldly.*) But I hardly see——

Bootle (*beginning to understand how he made the mistake*). A younger sister! Then you are Miss Prendergast? And my letter—Ah!

Enter Alice.

Alice. You are wanted, Jane, a moment.

Jane. Will you excuse me, Mr. Bootle?

(*Exit.*)

Bootle (*to Alice, as she follows her sister out*). Don't go!

Alice (*wanly, if she knows how*). Am I to stay and congratulate you?

Bootle. Alice! (*They approach the footlights, while* Jane, *having finished her business, comes in unobserved and watches from the back.*) It is all a mistake! I didn't know your Christian name—I didn't know you had a sister. The letter I addressed to Miss Prendergast I meant for Miss Alice Prendergast.

Alice. James! My love! But what can we do?

Bootle (*gloomily*). Nothing. As a man of honour I cannot withdraw. So two lives are ruined!

Alice. You are right, James. Jane must never know. Good-bye!

(*They give each other a farewell embrace.*)

Jane (*aside*). They love. (*Fiercely.*) But he is mine; I will hold him to his promise! (*Picking up a photograph of Alice as a small child from an occasional table.*) Little Alice! And I promised to take care of her—to protect her from the cruel world. Baby Alice! (*She puts her handkerchief to her eyes.*) No! I will not spoil two lives! (*Aloud.*) Why good-bye, Alice?

(Bootle *and* Alice, *who have been embracing all this time, unless they can think of something else to do, break away in surprise.*)

Alice. Jane—we—I——

Jane (*calmly*). Dear Alice! I understand perfectly. Mr. Bootle said in his letter to you that he was coming for his answer, and I see what answer you have given him. (*To* Bootle.) You remember I told you it would be "Yes." I know my little sister, you see.

Bootle (*tactlessly*). But—you told me I could kiss you!

Jane (*smiling*). And I tell you again now. I believe it is usual for men to kiss their sisters-in-law? (*She offers her cheek.* Bootle, *whose day it is, salutes her respectfully.*) And now (*gaily*) perhaps I had better leave you young people alone!

(*Exit, with a backward look at the audience expressive of the fact that she has been wearing the mask.*)

Bootle. Alice, then you are mine, after all!

Alice. James! (*They k—— No, perhaps better not. There has been quite enough for one evening.*) And to think that she knew all the time. Now I am quite, quite happy. And James—you *will* remember in future that I am Miss *Alice* Prendergast?

Bootle (*gaily*). My dear, I shall only be able to remember that you are The Future Mrs. Bootle!

CURTAIN.

XLIII. "AT DEAD OF NIGHT"

The stage is in semi-darkness as Dick Trayle *throws open the window from outside, puts his knee on the sill, and falls carefully into the drawing-room of Beeste Hall. He is dressed in a knickerbocker suit with arrows on it (such as can always be borrowed from a friend), and, to judge from the noises which he emits, is not in the best of training. The lights go on suddenly; and he should seize this moment to stagger to the door and turn on the switch. This done he sinks into the nearest chair and closes his eyes.*

If he has been dancing very late the night before, he may drop into a peaceful sleep; in which case the play ends here. Otherwise, no sooner are his eyes closed than he opens them with a sudden start and looks round in terror.

Dick (*striking the keynote at once*). No, no! Let me out—I am innocent! (*He gives a gasp of relief as he realises the situation.*) Free! It is true, then! I have escaped! I dreamed that I was back in prison again! (*He shudders and helps himself to a large whisky-and-soda, which he swallows at a gulp.*) That's better! Now I feel a new man—the man I was three years ago. Three years! It has been a lifetime! (*Pathetically to the audience.*) Where is Millicent now? (*The audience guesses that she is in the making-up room, but musn't say so.*) Alas! (*He falls into a reverie, from which he is suddenly wakened by a noise outside. He starts, and then creeps rapidly to the switch, arriving there at the moment when the lights go out. Then he goes swiftly behind the window curtain. The lights go up again as* Jasper Beeste *comes in with a revolver in one hand and a bull's-eye lantern of apparently enormous candle power in the other.*)

Jasper (*in immaculate evening dress*). I thought I heard a noise, so I slipped on some old things hurriedly and came down. (*Fingering his perfectly-tied tie.*) But there seems to be nobody here. (*Turns round suddenly to the window.*) Ha, who's there? Hands up, blow you (*he ought to swear rather badly here, really*) hands up or I fire!

(*The stage is suddenly plunged into darkness, there is the noise of a struggle, and the lights go on to reveal* Jasper *by the door covering* Dick *with his revolver.*)

Jasper. Let's have a little light on you. (*Brutally.*) Now then, my man, what have you got to say for yourself? Ha! An escaped convict, eh?

Dick (*to himself, in amazement*). Jasper Beeste!

Jasper. So you know my name?

Dick (*in the tones of a man whose whole life has been blighted by the machinations of a false friend*). Yes, Jasper Beeste, I know your name. For two years I have said it to myself every night, when I prayed Heaven that I should meet you again.

Jasper. Again? (*Uneasily.*) We have met before?

Dick (*slowly*). We have met before, Jasper Beeste. Since then I have lived a lifetime of misery. You may well fail to recognise me.

Enter Millicent Wilsdon—*in a dressing gown, with her hair over her shoulders, if the county will stand it.*

Millicent (*to Jasper*). I couldn't sleep—I heard a noise—I— (*suddenly seeing the other*) Dick! (*She trembles.*)

Dick. Millicent! (*He trembles too.*)

Jasper. Trayle! (*So does he.*)

Dick (*bitterly*). You shrink from me, Millicent. (*With strong common sense.*) What is an escaped convict to the beautiful Miss Wilsdon?

Millicent. Dick—I—you—when you were sentenced——

Dick. When I was sentenced—the evidence was black against me, I admit—I wrote and released you from your engagement. You are married now?

Millicent (*throwing herself on a sofa*). Oh, Dick!

Jasper (*recovering himself*). Enough of this. Miss Wilsdon is going to marry me to-morrow.

Dick. To marry *you*! (*He strides over to sofa and pulls Millicent to her feet.*) Millicent, look me in the eyes! Do you love him? (*She turns away.*) Say "Yes" and I will go back quietly to my prison. (*She raises her eyes to his.*) Ha! I thought so! You don't love him! Now then I can speak.

Jasper (*advancing threateningly*). Yes, to your friends, the warders. Millicent, ring the bell.

Dick (*wresting the revolver from his grasp*). Ha, would you? Now stand over there and listen to me. (*He arranges his audience,* Millicent *on a sofa on the right, Jasper, biting his finger nails, on the left.*) Three years ago Lady Wilsdon's diamond necklace was stolen. My flat was searched and the necklace was found in my hatbox. Although I protested my innocence I was tried, found guilty, and sentenced to ten years' penal servitude, followed by fifteen years' police supervision.

Millicent (*raising herself on the sofa*). Dick, you were innocent—I know it. (*She flops back again.*)

Dick. I was. But how could I prove it? I went to prison. For a year black despair gnawed at my heart. And then something happened. The prisoner in the cell next to mine tried to communicate with me by means of taps. We soon arranged a system and held conversations together. One day he told me of a robbery in which he and another man had been engaged—the robbery of a diamond necklace.

Jasper (*jauntily*). Well?

Dick (*sternly*). A diamond necklace, Jasper Beeste, which the other man hid in the hatbox of another man in order that he might woo the other man's *fiancée*! (Millicent *shrieks.*)

Jasper (*blusteringly*). Bah!

Dick (*quietly*). The man in the cell next to mine wants to meet this gentleman again. It seems that he has some old scores to pay off.

Jasper (*sneeringly*). And where is he?

Dick. Ah, where is he? (*He goes to the window and gives a low whistle. A stranger in knickerbockers jumps in and advances with a crab-like movement.*) Good! here you are. Allow me to present you to Mr. Jasper Beeste.

Jasper (*in horror*). Two-toed Thomas! I am undone!

Two-toed Thomas (*after a series of unintelligible snarls*). Say the word, guv'nor, and I'll kill him. (*He prowls round* Jasper *thoughtfully.*)

Dick (*sternly*). Stand back! Now, Jasper Beeste, what have you to say?

Jasper (*hysterically*). I confess. I will sign anything. I will go to prison. Only keep that man off me.

Dick (*going up to a bureau and writing aloud at incredible speed*). "I, Jasper Beeste, of Beeste Hall, do hereby declare that I stole Lady Wilsdon's diamond necklace and hid it in the hatbox of Richard Trayle; and I further declare that the said Richard Trayle is innocent of any complicity in the affair. (*Advancing with the paper and a fountain pen.*) Sign, please."

(*Jasper signs. At this moment two warders burst into the room.*)

First Warder. There they are!

(*He seizes* Dick. Two-toed Thomas *leaps from the window, pursued by the second Warder.* Millicent *picks up the confession and advances dramatically.*)

Millicent. Do not touch that man! Read this!

(*She hands him the confession with an air of superb pride.*)

First Warder (*reading*). Jasper Beeste! (*Slipping a pair of handcuffs on* Jasper.) You come along with me, my man. We've had our suspicions of you for some time. (*To* Millicent, *with a nod at* Dick). You'll look after that gentleman, miss?

Millicent. Of course! Why, he's engaged to me. Aren't you, Dick?

Dick. This time, Millicent, for ever!

CURTAIN.

XLIV. "THE LOST HEIRESS"

The Scene is laid outside a village inn in that county of curious dialects, Loamshire. The inn is easily indicated by a round table bearing two mugs of liquid, while a fallen log emphasises the rural nature of the scene. Gaffer Jarge *and* Gaffer Willyum *are seated at the table, surrounded by a fringe of whisker,* Jarge *being slightly more of a gaffer than* Willyum.

Jarge (*who missed his dinner through nervousness and has been ordered to sustain himself with soup—as he puts down the steaming mug*). Eh, bor but this be rare beer. So it be.

Willyum (*who had too much dinner and is now draining his liquid paraffin*). You be right, Gaffer Jarge. Her be main rare beer. (*He feels up his sleeve, but thinking better of it, wipes his mouth with the back of his hand.*) Main rare beer, zo her be. (*Gagging.*) Zure-lie.

Jarge. Did I ever tell 'ee, bor, about t' new squoire o' these parts—him wot cum hum yesterday from furren lands? Gaffer Henry wor a-telling me.

Willyum (*privately bored*). Thee didst tell 'un, lad, sartain sure thee didst. And Gaffer Henry, he didst tell 'un too. But tell 'un again. It du me good to hear 'un, zo it du. Zure-lie.

Jarge. A rackun it be a main queer tale, queerer nor any them writing chaps tell about. It wor like this. (*Dropping into English, in his hurry to get his long speech over before he forgets it.*) The old Squire had a daughter who disappeared when she was three weeks old, eighteen years ago. It was always thought she was stolen by somebody, and the Squire would have it that she was still alive. When he died a year ago he left the estate and all his money to a distant cousin in

Australia, with the condition that if he did not discover the missing baby within twelve months everything was to go to the hospitals. (*Remembering his smock and whiskers with a start.*) And here du be the last day, zo it be, and t' Squoire's daughter, her ain't found.

Willyum (*puffing at a new and empty clay pipe*). Zure-lie. (*Jarge, a trifle jealous of* Willyum's *gag, pulls out a similar pipe, but smokes it with the bowl upside down to show his independence.*) T' Squire's darter (*Jarge frowns*)—her bain't (*Jarge wishes he had thought of "bain't"*)—her bain't found. (*There is a dramatic pause, only broken by the prompter.*) Her ud be little Rachel's age now, bor?

Jarge (*reflectively*). Ay, ay. A main queer lass little Rachel du be. Her bain't like one of us.

Willyum. Her do be that fond of zoap and water. (*Laughter.*)

Jarge (*leaving nothing to chance*). Happen she might be a real grand lady by birth, bor.

Enter Rachel, *beautifully dressed in the sort of costume in which one would go to a fancy-dress ball as a village maiden.*

Rachel (*in the most expensive accent*). Now, Uncle George (*shaking a finger at him*), didn't you promise me you'd go straight home? It would serve you right if I never tied your tie for you again. (*She smiles brightly at him.*)

Jarge (*slapping his thigh in ecstasy*). Eh, lass! yer du keep us old uns in order. (*He bursts into a falsetto chuckle, loses the note, blushes and buries his head in his mug.*)

Willyum (*rising*). Us best be gettin' down along, Jarge, a rackun.

Jarge. Ay, bor, time us chaps was moving. Don't 'e be long, lass. (*Exeunt, limping heavily.*)

Rachel (*sitting down on the log*). Dear old men! How I love them all in this village! I have known it all my life. How strange it is that I have never had a father or mother. Sometimes I seem to remember a life different to this—a life in fine houses and spacious parks, among beautifully dressed people (*which is surprising seeing that she was only three weeks old at the time; but the audience must be given a hint of the plot*), and then it all fades away again. (*She looks fixedly into space.*)

Enter Hugh Fitzhugh, *Squire.*

Fitzhugh (*standing behind Rachel, but missing her somehow*). Did ever man come into stranger inheritance? A wanderer in Central Australia, I hear unexpectedly of my cousin's death through an advertisement in an old copy of a Sunday newspaper. I hasten home—too late to soothe his dying hours; too late indeed to enjoy my good fortune for more than one short day. To-morrow I must give up all to the hospitals, unless by some stroke of Fate this missing girl turns up. (*Impatiently.*) Pshaw! She is dead. (*Suddenly he notices* Rachel.) By heaven, a pretty girl in this out-of-the-way village! (*He walks round her.*) Gad, she is lovely! Hugh, my boy, you are in luck. (*He takes off his hat.*) Good evening, my dear!

Rachel (*with a start*). Good evening.

Fitzhugh (*aside*). She is adorable. She can be no common village wench. (*Aloud.*) Do you live here, my girl?

Rachel. Yes, I have always lived here. (*Aside.*) How handsome he is. Down, fluttering heart.

Fitzhugh (*sitting on the log beside her*). And who is the lucky village lad who is privileged to woo such beauty?

Rachel. I have no lover, Sir.

Fitzhugh (*taking her hand*). Can Hodge be so blind?

Rachel (*innocently*). Are you making love to me?

Fitzhugh. Upon my word I—(*He gets up from the log, which is not really comfortable.*) What is your name?

Rachel. Rachel. (*She rises.*)

Fitzhugh. It is the most beautiful name in the world. Rachel, will you be my wife?

Rachel. But we have known each other such a short time!

Fitzhugh (*lying bravely*). We have known each other for ever.

Rachel. And you are a rich gentleman, while I——

Fitzhugh. A gentleman, I hope, but rich—no. To-morrow I shall be a beggar. No, not a beggar if I have your love, Rachel.

Rachel (*making a lucky shot at his name*). Hugh! (*They embrace.*)

Fitzhugh. Let us plight our troth here. See, I give you my ring!

Rachel. And I give you mine.

(*She takes one from the end of a chain which is round her neck, and puts it on his finger. Fitzhugh looks at it and staggers back.*)

Fitzhugh. Heavens! They are the same ring! (*In great excitement.*) Child, child, who are you? How came you by the crest of the Fitzhughs?

Rachel. Ah, who am I? I never had any parents. When they found me they found that ring on me, and I have kept it ever since!

Fitzhugh. Let me look at you! It must be! The Squire's missing daughter!

(Gaffers Jarge *and* Willyum, *having entered unobserved at the back some time ago, have been putting in a lot of heavy by-play until wanted.*)

Jarge (*at last*). Lor' bless 'ee, Willyum, if it bain't Squire a-kissin' our Rachel.

Willyum. Zo it du be. Here du be goings-on! What will t' passon say?

Jarge (*struck with an idea*). Zay, bor, don't 'ee zee a zort o' loikeness atween t' maid and t' Squire?

Willyum. Jarge, if you bain't right, lad. Happen she do have t' same nose!

(*Hearing something,* Fitzhugh *and* Rachel *turn round.*)

Fitzhugh. Ah, my men! I'm your new Squire. Do you know who this is?

Willyum. Why, her du be our Rachel.

Fitzhugh. On the contrary, allow me to introduce you to Miss Fitzhugh, daughter of the late Squire!

Jarge. Well, this du be a day! To think of our Rachel now!

Fitzhugh. *My* Rachel now!

Rachel (*who, it is to be hoped, has been amusing herself somehow since her last speech*). Your Rachel always.

CURTAIN.

XLV. "THE LITERARY LIFE"

The Scene is the Editor's room in the Office of "The Lark." Two walls of the room are completely hidden from floor to ceiling by magnificently bound books; the third wall at the back is hidden by boxes of immensely expensive cigars. The windows, of course, are in the fourth wall, which, however, need not be described, as it is never quite practicable on the stage. The floor of this apartment is chastely covered with rugs shot by the Editor in his travels, or in the Tottenham Court Road; or, in some cases, presented by admiring readers from abroad. The furniture is both elegant and commodious.

William Smith, Editor, comes in. He is superbly dressed in a fur coat and an expensive cigar. There is a blue pencil behind his ear, and a sheaf of what we call in the profession "typewritten manuscripts" under his arm. He sitsdown at his desk and pulls the telephone towards him.

Smith (*at the telephone*). Hallo, is that you, Jones?... Yes, it's me. Just come up a moment. (*Puts down telephone and begins to open his letters.*)

Enter Jones, his favourite sub-editor. He is dressed quite commonly, and is covered with ink. He salutes respectfully as he comes into the room.

Jones. Good afternoon, chief.

Smith. Good afternoon. Have a cigar?

Jones. Thank you, chief.

Smith. Have you anything to tell me?

Jones. The circulation is still going up, chief. It was three million and eight last week.

Smith (*testily*). How often have I told you not to call me "chief," except when there are ladies present? Why can't you do what you're told?

Jones. Sorry, sir, but the fact is there are ladies present.

Smith (*fingering his moustache*). Show them up. Who are they?

Jones. There is only one. She says she's the lady who has been writing our anonymous "Secrets of the Boudoir" series which has made such a sensation.

Smith (in amazement). I thought you told me *you* wrote those.

Jones (simply). I did.

Smith. Then why——

Jones. I mean I did tell you. The truth is they came in anonymously, and I thought they were more likely to be accepted if I said I had written them. (*With great emotion.*) Forgive me, chief, but it was for the paper's sake. (*In matter-of-fact tones.*) There were one or two peculiarities of style I had to alter. She had a way of——

Smith (*sternly*). How many cheques for them have you accepted for the paper's sake?

Jones. Eight. For a thousand pounds each.

Smith (*with tears in his eyes*). If your mother were to hear of this——
——

Jones (*sadly*). Ah, chief, I never had a mother.

Smith (*slightly put out, but recovering himself quickly*). What would your father say if——

Jones. Alas, I have no relations. I was a foundling.

Smith (*nettled*). In that case I shall certainly tell the master of your workhouse. To think that there should be a thief in this office.

Jones (*with great pathos*). Chief, chief, I am not so vile as that. I have carefully kept all the cheques in an old stocking, and——

Smith (*in surprise*). Do you wear stockings?

Jones When I bicycle. And as soon as the contributor comes forward——

Smith (*stretching out his hand and grasping that of Jones*). My dear boy, forgive me. You have been hasty, perhaps, but zealous. In any case, your honesty is above suspicion. Leave me now. I have much to think of. (*Rests his head on his hands. Then, dreamily.*) You have never seen your father; for thirty years *I* have not seen my wife.... Ah, Arabella!

Jones. Yes, sir. (*Rings bell.*)

Smith. She *would* split her infinitives.... We quarrelled.... She left me.... I have never seen her again.

Jones (*excitedly*). Did you say she split her infinitives?

Smith. Yes. That was what led to our separation. Why?

Jones. Nothing, only—it's very odd. I wonder——

Enter Boy.

Boy. Did you ring, Sir?

Smith. No. But you can show the lady up. (*Exit* Boy.) You'd better clear out, Jones. I'll explain to her about the money.

Smith. Right you are, Sir. (*Exit.*)

(Smith *leans back in his chair and stares in front of him.*)

Smith (*to himself*). Arabella!

Enter Boy, *followed by a stylishly dressed lady of middle age.*

Boy. Mrs. Robinson. (*Exit.*)

(Mrs. Robinson *stops short in the middle of the room and stares at the Editor; then staggers and drops on to the sofa.*)

Smith (*in wonder*). Arabella!

Mrs. Robinson. William!

(*They fall into each other's arms.*)

Arabella. I had begun to almost despair. (*Smith winces.*) "Almost to despair," I mean, darling.

Smith (*with a great effort*). No, no, dear. You were right.

Arabella. How sweet of you to think so, William.

Smith. Yes, yes, it's the least I can say.... I have been very lonely without you, dear.... And now, what shall we do? Shall we get married again quietly?

Arabella. Wouldn't that be bigamy?

Smith. I think not, but I will ask the printer's reader. He knows everything. You see, there will be such a lot to explain, otherwise.

Arabella. Dear, can you afford to marry?

Smith. Well, my salary as editor is only twenty thousand a year, but I do a little reviewing for other papers.

Arabella. And I have—nothing. How can I come to you without even a trousseau?

Smith. Yes, that's true.... (*Suddenly*) By Jove, though, you *have* got something! You have eight thousand pounds! We owe you that for your articles. (*With a return to his professional manner.*) Did I tell you how greatly we all appreciated them? (*Goes to telephone.*) Is that you, Jones? Just come here a moment. (*To* Arabella) Jones is my sub-editor; he is keeping your money for you.

Enter Jones.

Jones (*producing an old stocking*). I've just been round to my rooms to get that money—(*sees* Arabella)—oh, I beg your pardon.

Smith (*waving an introduction*). Mrs. Smith—my wife. This is our sub-editor, dear—Mr. Jones. (*Arabella puts her hand to her heart and seems about to faint.*) Why, what's the matter?

Arabella (*hoarsely*). Where did you get that stocking?

Smith (*pleasantly*). It's one he wears when he goes bicycling.

Jones. No; I misled you this afternoon, chief. This stocking was all the luggage I had when I first entered the Leamington workhouse.

Arabella (*throwing herself into his arms*). My son! This is your father! William—our boy!

Smith (*shaking hands with Jones*). How are you? I say, Arabella, then that was one of *my* stockings?

Arabella (*to her boy.*) When I saw you on the stairs you seemed to dimly remind me——

Jones. To remind you dimly, mother.

Smith. No, my boy. In future, nothing but split infinitives will appear in our paper. Please remember that.

Jones (*with emotion*). I will endeavour to always remember it, dad.

CURTAIN.

SUCCESSFUL MEN

[*This series is designed to assist parents in choosing a career for their sons. The author has devoted considerable time to research among the best authorities, and the results are now laid before the public in the hope that they will bring encouragement to those who are hesitating at the doors of any of the great professions.*]

XLVI. THE SOLICITOR

The office was at its busiest, for it was Friday afternoon. John Blunt leant back in his comfortable chair and toyed with the key of the safe, while he tried to realise his new position. He, John Blunt, was junior partner in the great London firm of Macnaughton, Macnaughton, Macnaughton, Macnaughton & Macnaughton.

He closed his eyes, and his thoughts wandered back to the day when he had first entered the doors of the firm as one of two hundred and seventy-eight applicants for the post of office-boy. They had been interviewed in batches, and old Mr. Sanderson, the senior partner, had taken the first batch.

"I like your face, my boy," he had said heartily to John.

"And I like yours," replied John, not to be outdone in politeness.

"Now I wonder if you can spell 'mortgage'?"

"One 'm,'" said John tentatively.

Mr. Sanderson was delighted with the lad's knowledge, and engaged him at once.

For three years John had done his duty faithfully. During this time he had saved the firm more than once by his readiness—particularly on one occasion, when he had called old Mr. Sanderson's attention to the fact that he had signed a letter to a firm of stockbrokers, "Your loving husband, Macnaughton, Macnaughton, Macnaughton, Macnaughton & Macnaughton." Mr. Sanderson, always a little absent-minded, corrected the error, and promised the boy his articles. Five years later John Blunt was a solicitor.

And now he was actually junior partner in the firm—the firm of which it was said in the City, "If a man has Macnaughton, Macnaughton, Macnaughton, Macnaughton & Macnaughton behind him he is all right." The City is always coining pithy little epigrams like this.

There was a knock at the door of the enquiry office and a prosperous-looking gentleman came in.

"Can I see Mr. Macnaughton?" he said politely to the office-boy.

"There isn't no Mr. Macnaughton," replied the latter. "They all died years ago."

"Well, well, can I see one of the partners?"

"You can't see Mr. Sanderson, because he's having his lunch," said the boy. "Mr. Thorpe hasn't come back from lunch yet, Mr. Peters has just gone out to lunch, Mr. Williams is expected back from lunch every minute, Mr. Gourlay went out to lunch an hour ago, Mr. Beamish——"

"Tut, tut, isn't anybody in?"

"Mr. Blunt is in," said the boy, and took up the telephone. "If you wait a moment I'll see if he's awake."

Half an hour later Mr. Masters was shown into John Blunt's room.

"I'm sorry I was engaged," said John. "A most important client. Now what can I do for you, Mr.—er—Masters?"

"I wish to make my will."

"By all means," said John cordially.

"I have only one child, to whom I intend to leave all my money."

"Ha!" said John, with a frown. "This will be a lengthy and difficult business."

"But you can do it?" asked Mr. Masters anxiously. "They told me at the hairdresser's that Macnaughton, Macnaughton, Macnaughton, Macnaughton & Macnaughton was the cleverest firm in London."

"We can do it," said John simply, "but it will require all our care; and I think it would be best if I were to come and stay with you for the week-end. We could go into it properly then."

"Thank you," said Mr. Masters, clasping the other's hand. "I was just going to suggest it. My motor-car is outside. Let us go at once."

"I will follow you in a moment," said John, and, pausing only to snatch a handful of money from the safe for incidental expenses and to tell the boy that he would be back on Monday, he picked up the well-filled week-end bag which he always kept ready, and hurried after the other.

Inside the car Mr. Masters was confidential.

"My daughter," he said, "comes of age to-morrow."

"Oh, it's a daughter?" said John in surprise. "Is she pretty?"

"She is considered to be the prettiest girl in the county."

"Really?" said John. He thought a moment, and added, "Can we stop at a post-office? I must send an important business telegram." He took out a form and wrote "Macmacmacmacmac, London. Shall not be back till Wednesday. Blunt."

The car stopped and then sped on again.

"Amy has never been any trouble to me," said Mr. Masters, "but I am getting old now, and I would give a thousand pounds to see her happily married."

"To whom would you give it?" asked John, whipping out his pocket-book.

"Tut, tut, a mere figure of speech. But I would settle a hundred thousand pounds on her on the wedding-day."

"Indeed?" said John thoughtfully. "Can we stop at another post-office?" he added, bringing out his fountain-pen again.

He took out a second telegraph form and wrote:

"Macmacmacmacmac, London. Shall not be back till Friday. Blunt."

The car dashed on again, and an hour later arrived at a commodious mansion standing in its own well-timbered grounds of upwards of several acres. At the front door a graceful figure was standing.

"My solicitor, dear, Mr. Blunt," said Mr. Masters.

"It is very good of you to come all this way on my father's business," she said shyly.

"Not at all," said John. "A week or—or a fortnight—or——" he looked at her again—"or—three weeks, and the thing is done."

"Is making a will so very difficult?"

"It's a very tricky and complicated affair indeed. However, I think we shall pull it off. Er—might I send an important business telegram?"

"Macmacmacmacmacmac, London," wrote John. "Very knotty case. Date of return uncertain. Please send more cash for incidental expenses. Blunt."

Yes, you have guessed what happened. It is an every-day experience in a solicitor's life. John Blunt and Amy Masters were married at St. George's, Hanover Square, last May. The wedding was a quiet one owing to mourning in the bride's family—the result of a too sudden perusal of Macnaughton, Macnaughton, Macnaughton, Macnaughton & Macnaughton's bill of costs. As Mr. Masters said with his expiring breath: he didn't mind paying for our Mr. Blunt's skill; nor yet for our Mr. Blunt's valuable time—even if most of it was spent in courting Amy; nor, again, for our Mr. Blunt's tips to servants; but he did object to being charged the first-class railway fare both ways when our Mr.[Pg 355] Blunt had come down and gone up again in the car. And perhaps I ought to add that that is the drawback to this fine profession. One is so often misunderstood.

XLVII. THE PAINTER

Mr. Paul Samways was in a mood of deep depression. The artistic temperament is peculiarly given to these moods, but in Paul's case there was reason why he should take a gloomy view of things. His masterpiece, "The Shot Tower from Battersea Bridge," together with the companion picture "Battersea Bridge from the Shot Tower," had been purchased by a dealer for seventeen and sixpence. His sepia monochrome, "Night," had brought him an I.O.U. for five shillings. These were his sole earnings for the last six weeks, and starvation stared him in the face.

"If only I had a little capital!" he cried aloud in despair. "Enough to support me until my Academy picture is finished." His Academy picture was a masterly study entitled, "Roll on, thou deep and dark blue ocean, roll," and he had been compelled to stop halfway across the Channel through sheer lack of ultramarine.

The clock struck two, reminding him that he had not lunched. He rose wearily and went to the little cupboard which served as a larder. There was but little there to make a satisfying meal—half a loaf of bread, a corner of cheese, and a small tube of Chinese white. Mechanically he set the things out....

He had finished and was clearing away when there came a knock at the door. His charwoman, whose duty it was to clean his brushes every week, came in with a card.

"A lady to see you, Sir," she said.

Paul read the card in astonishment.

"The Duchess of Winchester," he exclaimed. "What on earth—Show her in, please." Hastily picking up a brush and the first tube which came to hand, he placed himself in a dramatic position before his easel and set to work.

"How do you do, Mr. Samways?" said the Duchess.

"G-good afternoon," said Paul, embarrassed both by the presence of a duchess in his studio and by his sudden discovery that he was touching up a sunset with a tube of carbolic tooth paste.

"Our mutual friend, Lord Ernest Topwood, recommended me to come to you."

Paul, who had never met Lord Ernest, but had once seen his name in a ha'penny paper beneath a photograph of Mr. Arnold Bennett, bowed silently.

"As you probably guess, I want you to paint my daughter's portrait."

Paul opened his mouth to say that he was only a landscape painter, and then closed it again. After all, it was hardly fair to bother her Grace with technicalities.

"I hope you can undertake this commission," she said pleadingly.

"I shall be delighted," said Paul. "I am rather busy just now, but I could begin at two o'clock on Monday."

"Excellent," said the Duchess. "Till Monday, then." And Paul, still clutching the tooth paste, conducted her to her carriage.

Punctually at 3.15 on Monday Lady Hermione appeared. Paul drew a deep breath of astonishment when he saw her, for she was lovely beyond compare. All his skill as a landscape painter would be needed if he were to do justice to her beauty. As quickly as possible he placed her in position and set to work....

"May I let my face go for a moment?" said Lady Hermione after three hours of it.

"Yes, let us stop," said Paul. He had outlined her in charcoal and burnt cork, and it would be too dark to do any more that evening.

"Tell me where you first met Lord Ernest?" she asked, as she came down to the fire.

"At the Savoy in June," said Paul boldly.

Lady Hermione laughed merrily. Paul, who had not regarded his last remark as one of his best things, looked at her in surprise.

"But your portrait of him was in the Academy in May!" she smiled.

Paul made up his mind quickly.

"Lady Hermione," he said with gravity, "do not speak to me of Lord Ernest again. Nor," he added hurriedly, "to Lord Ernest of me. When your picture is finished I will tell you why. Now it is time you went." He woke the Duchess up, and made a few commonplace remarks about the weather. "Remember," he whispered to Lady Hermione as he saw them to their car. She nodded and smiled.

The sittings went on daily. Sometimes Paul would paint rapidly with great sweeps of the brush; sometimes he would spend an hour trying to get on his palette the exact shade of green bice for the famous Winchester emeralds; sometimes in despair he would take a sponge and wipe the whole picture out, and then start madly again. And sometimes he would stop work altogether and tell Lady Hermione about his home-life in Worcestershire. But always, when he woke the Duchess up at the end of the sitting, he would say "Remember!" and Lady Hermione would nod back at him.

It was a spring-like day in March when the picture was finished, and nothing remained to do but to paint in the signature.

"It is beautiful!" said Lady Hermione, with enthusiasm. "Beautiful! Is it at all like me?"

Paul looked from her to the picture, and back to her again.

"No," he said. "Not a bit. You know, I am really a landscape painter."

"What do you mean?" she cried. "You are Peter Samways, A.R.A., the famous portrait painter!"

"No," he said sadly. "That was my secret. I am Paul Samways. A member of the Amateur Rowing Association, it is true, but only an unknown landscape painter. Peter Samways lives in the next studio, and he is not even a relation."

"Then you have deceived me! You have brought me here under false pretences!" She stamped her foot angrily. "My father will not buy that picture, and I forbid you to exhibit it as a portrait of myself."

"My dear Lady Hermione," said Paul, "you need not be alarmed. I propose to exhibit the picture as 'When the Heart is Young.' Nobody will recognise a likeness to you in it. And if the Duke does not buy it I have no doubt that some other purchaser will come along."

Lady Hermione looked at him thoughtfully. "Why did you do it?" she asked gently.

"Because I fell in love with you."

She dropped her eyes, and then raised them gaily to his. "Mother is still asleep," she whispered.

"Hermione!" he cried, dropping his palette and putting his brush behind his ear.

She held out her arms to him.

As everybody remembers, "When the Heart is Young," by Paul Samways, was the feature of the Exhibition. It was bought for £10,000 by a retired bottle-manufacturer, whom it reminded a little of his late mother. Paul woke to find himself famous. But the success which began for him from this day did not spoil his simple and generous nature. He never forgot his brother artists, whose feet were not yet on the top of the ladder. Indeed one of his first acts after he was married was to give a commission to Peter Samways, A.R.A.— nothing less than the painting of his wife's portrait. And Lady Hermione was delighted with the result.

XLVIII. THE BARRISTER

The New Bailey was crowded with a gay and fashionable throng. It was a remarkable case of shop-lifting. Aurora Delaine, 19, was charged with feloniously stealing and conveying certain articles the property of the Universal Stores, to wit, thirty-five yards of book muslin, ten pairs of gloves, a sponge, two gimlets, five jars of cold cream, a copy of the Clergy List, three hat-guards, a mariner's compass, a box of drawing-pins, an egg-breaker, six blouses, and a cabman's whistle. The theft had been proved by Albert Jobson, a shopwalker, who gave evidence to the effect that he followed her through the different departments and saw her take the things mentioned in the indictment.

"Just a moment," interrupted the Judge. "Who is defending the prisoner?"

There was an unexpected silence. Rupert Carleton, who had dropped idly into court, looked round in sudden excitement. The poor girl had no counsel! What if he—yes, he would seize the chance! He stood up boldly. "I am, my Lord," he said.

Rupert Carleton was still in the twenties, but he had been a briefless barrister for some years. Yet, though briefs would not come, he had been very far from idle. He had stood for Parliament in both the Conservative and Liberal interests (not to mention his own), he had written half-a-dozen unproduced plays, and he was engaged to be married. But success in his own profession had been delayed. Now at last was his opportunity.

He pulled his wig down firmly over his ears, took out a pair of *pince-nez* and rose to cross-examine. It was the cross-examination which was to make him famous, the cross-examination which is now given as a model in every legal text-book.

"Mr. Jobson," he began suavely, "you say that you saw the accused steal these various articles, and that they were afterwards found upon her?"

"Yes."

"I put it to you," said Rupert, and waited intently for the answer, "that that is a pure invention on your part?"

"No."

With a superhuman effort Rupert hid his disappointment. Unexpected as the answer was, he preserved his impassivity.

"I suggest," he tried again, "that you followed her about and concealed this collection of things in her cloak with a view to advertising your winter sale?"

"No. I saw her steal them."

Rupert frowned; the man seemed impervious to the simplest suggestion. With masterly decision he tapped his *pince-nez* and fell back upon his third line of defence. "You saw her steal them? What you mean is that you saw her take them from the different counters and put them in her bag?"

"Yes."

"With the intention of paying for them in the ordinary way?"

"No."

"Please be very careful. You said in your evidence that prisoner when told she would be charged, cried, 'To think that I should have come to this! Will no one save me?' I suggest that she went up to you with her collection of purchases, pulled out her purse, and said, 'What does all this come to? I can't get any one to serve me.'"

"No."

The obstinacy of some people! Rupert put back his *pince-nez* in his pocket and brought out another pair. The historic cross-examination continued.

"We will let that pass for the moment," he said. He consulted a blank sheet of paper and then looked sternly at Mr. Jobson. "Mr. Jobson, how many times have you been married?"

"Once."

"Quite so." He hesitated and then decided to risk it. "I suggest that your wife left you?"

"Yes."

It was a long shot, but once again the bold course had paid. Rupert heaved a sigh of relief.

"Will you tell the gentlemen of the jury," he said with deadly politeness, "*why* she left you."

"She died."

A lesser man might have been embarrassed, but Rupert's iron nerve did not fail him.

"Exactly!" he said. "And was that or was that not on the night when you were turned out of the Hampstead Parliament for intoxication?"

"I never was."

"Indeed? Will you cast your mind back to the night of April 24th, 1897? What were you doing on that night?"

"I have no idea," said Jobson, after casting his mind back and waiting in vain for some result.

"In that case you cannot swear that you were not being turned out of the Hampstead Parliament——"

"But I never belonged to it."

Rupert leaped at the damaging admission.

"What? You told the Court you lived at Hampstead, and yet you say that you never belonged to the Hampstead Parliament? Is *that* your idea of patriotism?"

"I said I lived at Hackney."

"To the Hackney Parliament, I should say. I am suggesting that you were turned out of the Hackney Parliament——"

"I don't belong to that either."

"Exactly!" said Rupert triumphantly. "Having been turned out for intoxication?"

"And never did belong."

"Indeed? May I take it then that you prefer to spend your evenings in the public-house?"

"If you want to know," said Jobson angrily, "I belong to the Hackney Chess Circle, and that takes up most of my evenings."

Rupert gave a sigh of satisfaction and turned to the jury.

"*At last*, gentlemen, we have got it. I thought we should arrive at the truth in the end, in spite of Mr. Jobson's prevarications." He turned to the witness. "Now, Sir," he said sternly, "you have already told the Court that you have no idea what you were doing on the night of April 24th, 1897. I put it to you once more that this blankness of memory is due to the fact that you were in a state of intoxication on the premises of the Hackney Chess Circle. Can you swear on your oath that this is not so?"

A murmur of admiration for the relentless way in which the truth had been tracked down ran through the Court. Rupert drew himself up and put on both pairs of *pince-nez* at once.

"Come, Sir!" he said; "the jury is waiting."

But it was not Albert Jobson who answered. It was the counsel for the prosecution. "My lord," he said, getting up slowly, "this has come as a complete surprise to me. In the circumstances I must advise my clients to withdraw from the case."

"A very proper decision," said his lordship. "The prisoner is discharged without a stain on her character."

Briefs poured in upon Rupert next day, and he was engaged for all the big Chancery cases. Within a week his six plays were accepted, and within a fortnight he had entered Parliament as the miners' Member for Coalville. His marriage took place at the end of a month. The wedding presents were even more numerous and costly than usual, and included thirty-five yards of book-muslin, ten pairs of gloves, a sponge, two gimlets, five jars of cold cream, a copy of the Clergy List, three hat guards, a mariner's compass, a box of drawing-pins, an egg-breaker, six blouses, and a cabman's whistle. They were marked quite simply, "From a grateful friend."

XLIX. THE CIVIL SERVANT

It was three o'clock, and the afternoon sun reddened the western windows of one of the busiest of Government offices. In an airy room on the third floor Richard Dale was batting. Standing in front of the coal-box with the fire-shovel in his hands he was a model of the strenuous young Englishman; and as for the third time he turned the Government india-rubber neatly in the direction of square-leg and so completed his fifty the bowler could hardly repress a sigh of envious admiration. Even the reserved Matthews, who was too old for cricket, looked up a moment from his putting and said, "Well played, Dick!"

The fourth occupant of the room was busy at his desk, as if to give the lie to the thoughtless accusation that the Civil Service cultivates the body at the expense of the mind. The eager shouts of the players seemed to annoy him, for he frowned and bit his pen, or else passed his fingers restlessly through his hair.

"How the dickens do you expect any one to think in this confounded noise?" he cried suddenly.

"What's the matter, Ashby?"

"You're the matter. How am I going to get these verses done for *The Evening Surprise* if you make such a row? Why don't you go out to tea?"

"Good idea. Come on, Dale. You coming, Matthews?" They went out, leaving the room to Ashby.

In his youth Harold Ashby had often been told by his relations that he had a literary bent. His letters home from school were generally pronounced to be good enough for *Punch* and some of them, together with a certificate of character from his Vicar, were actually sent to that paper. But as he grew up he realised that his genius was better fitted for work of a more solid character. His post in the Civil Service gave him full leisure for his *Adam: A Fragment*, his *History of the Microscope*, and his *Studies in Rural Campanology*, and yet left him ample time in which to contribute to the journalism of the day.

The poem he was now finishing for *The Evening Surprise* was his first contribution to that paper, but he had little doubt that it would be accepted. It was called quite simply "Love and Death," and it began like this:

Love!O love!(All other things above).—Why,O why,Am I afraid to die?

There were six more lines which I have forgotten, but I suppose they gave the reason for this absurd diffidence.

Having written the poem out neatly, Harold put it in an envelope and took it round to *The Evening Surprise*. The strain of composition had left him rather weak, and he decided to give his brain a rest for the next few days. So it happened that he was at the wickets on the following Wednesday afternoon when the commissionaire brought him in the historic letter. He opened it hastily, the shovel under his arm.

"Dear Sir," wrote the editor of *The Evening Surprise*, "will you come round and see me as soon as convenient?"

Harold lost no time. Explaining that he would finish his innings later, he put his coat on, took his hat and stick, and dashed out.

"How do you do?" said the editor. "I wanted to talk to you about your work. We all liked your little poem very much. It will be coming out to-morrow."

"Thursday," said Harold helpfully.

"I was wondering whether we couldn't get you to join our staff. Does the idea of doing Aunt Miriam's Cosy Corner in our afternoon edition appeal to you at all?"

"No," said Harold. "Not a bit."

"Ah, that's a pity." He tapped his desk thoughtfully. "Well, then, how would you like to be a war correspondent?"

"Very much," said Harold. "I was considered to write rather good letters home from school."

"Splendid! There's this little war in Mexico. When can you start? All expenses and fifty pounds a week. You're not very busy at the office just now, I suppose?"

"I could get sick leave easily enough," said Harold, "if it wasn't for more than eight or nine months."

"Do; that will be excellent. Here's a blank cheque for your outfit. Can you get off to-morrow? But I suppose you'll have one or two things to finish up at the office first?"

"Well," said Harold cautiously, "I *was* in, and I'd made ninety-six. But if I go back and finish my innings now, and then have to-morrow for buying things, I could get off on Friday."

"Good," said the editor. "Well, here's luck. Come back alive if you can, and if you do we shan't forget you."

Harold spent the next day buying a war correspondent's outfit: the camel, the travelling bath, the putties, the pith helmet, the quinine, the sleeping-bag, and the thousand-and-one other necessities of active service. On the Friday his colleagues at the office came down in a body to Southampton to see him off. Little did they think that nearly a year would elapse before he again set foot upon England.

I shall not describe all his famous *coups* at Mexico. Sufficient to say that experience taught him quickly all that he had need to learn; and that whereas he was more than a week late with his cabled account of the first engagement of the war he was frequently more than a week early afterwards. Indeed the battle of Parson's Nose, so realistically described in his last telegram, is still waiting to be fought. It is to be hoped that it will be in time for his aptly-named book, *With the Mexicans in Mexico*, which is coming out next month.

On his return to England Harold found that time had wrought many changes. To begin with, the editor of *The Evening Surprise* had passed on to *The Morning Exclamation*.

"You had better take his place," said the ducal proprietor to Harold.

"Right," said Harold. "I suppose I shall have to resign my post at the office?"

"Just as you like. I don't see why you should."

"I should miss the cricket," said Harold wistfully, "and the salary. I'll go round see what I can arrange."

But there were also changes at the office. Harold had been rising steadily in salary and seniority during his absence, and he found to his delight that he was now a Principal Clerk. He found too that he

284

had acquired quite a reputation in the office for quickness and efficiency in his new work.

The first thing to arrange about was his holiday. He had had no holiday for more than a year, and there were some eight weeks owing to him.

"Hullo," said the Assistant Secretary as Harold came in, "you're looking well. I suppose you can manage to get away for the week-ends?"

"I've been away on sick leave for some time," said Harold pathetically.

"Have you? You've kept it very secret. Come out and have lunch with me, and we'll do a *matinée* afterwards."

Harold went out with him happily. It would be pleasant to accept the editorship of *The Evening Surprise* without giving up the Governmental work which was so dear to him, and the Assistant Secretary's words made this possible, for a year or so anyhow. Then, when his absence from the office began to be noticed, it would be time to think of retiring on an adequate pension.

L. THE ACTOR

Mr. Levinski, the famous actor-manager, dragged himself from beneath the car, took the snow out of his mouth, and swore heartily. Mortal men are liable to motor accidents; even king's cars have backfired; but it seems strange that actor-managers are not specially exempt from these occurrences. Mr. Levinski was not only angry; he was also a little shocked. When an actor-manager has to walk two miles to the nearest town on a winter evening, one may be pardoned a doubt as to whether all is quite right with the world.

But the completest tragedy has its compensations for some one. The pitiable arrival of Mr. Levinski at "The Duke's Head," unrecognised and with his fur coat slightly ruffled, might make a sceptic of the most devout optimist, and yet Eustace Merrowby can never look back upon that evening without a sigh of thankfulness; for to him it was the beginning of his career. The story has often been told since—in about a dozenweekly papers, half-a-dozen daily papers and three dozen provincial papers—but it will always bear telling again.

There was no train to London that night, and Mr. Levinski had been compelled to put up at "The Duke's Head." However, he had dined and was feeling slightly better. He summoned the manager of the hotel.

"What does one do in this damn place?" he asked with a yawn.

The manager, instantly recognising that he was speaking to a member of the aristocracy, made haste to reply. "Othello" was being played at the town theatre. His daughter, who had already been three times, told him that it was very sweet. He was sure his lordship....

Mr. Levinski dismissed him, and considered the point. He had to amuse himself with something that evening, and the choice apparently lay between "Othello" and the local Directory. He picked up the Directory. By a lucky chance for Eustace Merrowby it was three years old. Mr. Levinski put on his fur coat and went to see "Othello."

For some time he was as bored as he had expected to be, but halfway through the Third Act he began to wake up. There was something in the playing of the principal actor which moved him strangely. He looked at his programme. "*Othello*—MR. EUSTACE MERROWBY." Mr. Levinski frowned thoughtfully. "Merrowby," he said to himself. "I don't know the name, but he's the man I want." He took out the gold pencil presented to him by the Emperor—(the station-master had had a tie-pin)—and wrote a note.

He was finishing breakfast next morning when Mr. Merrowby was announced.

"Ah, good morning," said Mr. Levinski, "good morning. You find me very busy," and here he began to turn the pages of the Directory backwards and forwards, "but I can give you a moment. What is it you want?"

"You asked me to call on you," said Eustace.

"Did I, did I?" He passed his hand across his brow with a noble gesture. "I am so busy I forget. Ah, now I remember. I saw you play *Othello* last night. You are the man I want. I am producing 'Oom Baas,' the great South African drama, next April, at my theatre. Perhaps you know?"

"I have read about it in the papers," said Eustace. In all the papers (he might have added) every day, for the last six months.

"Good. Then you may have heard that one of the scenes is an ostrich farm. I want you to play 'Tommy.'"

"One of the ostriches?" asked Eustace.

"I do not offer the part of an ostrich to a man who has played *Othello*. Tommy is the Kaffir boy who looks after the farm. It is a black part, like your present one, but not so long. In London you cannot expect to take the leading parts just yet."

"This is very kind of you," said Eustace gratefully. "I have always longed to get to London. And to start in your theatre!—it's a wonderful chance."

"Good," said Mr. Levinski. "Then that's settled." He waved Eustace away and took up the Directory again with a business-like air.

And so Eustace Merrowby came to London. It is a great thing for a young actor to come to London. As Mr. Levinski had warned him, his new part was not so big as that of *Othello*; he had to say "Hofo tsetse!"—which was alleged to be Kaffir for "Down, Sir!" to the big ostrich. But to be at the St. George's Theatre at all was an honour which most men would envy him, and his association with a real ostrich was boundx to bring him before the public in the pages of the illustrated papers.

Eustace, curiously enough, was not very nervous on the first night. He was fairly certain that he was word-perfect; and if only the ostrich didn't kick him in the back of the neck—as it had tried to once at rehearsal—the evening seemed likely to be a triumph for him. And so it was with a feeling of pleasurable anticipation that, on the morning after, he gathered the papers round him at breakfast, and prepared to read what the critics had to say.

He had a remarkable Press. I give a few examples of the notices he obtained from the leading papers:

"Mr. Eustace Merrowby was Tommy."—*Daily Telegraph.*

"The cast included Mr. Eustace Merrowby."—*Times.*

" ... Mr. Eustace Merrowby ... "—*Daily Chronicle.*

"We have no space in which to mention all the other performers."—*Morning Leader.*

"This criticism only concerns the two actors we have mentioned, and does not apply to the rest of the cast."—*Sportsman.*

"Where all were so good it would be invidious to single out anybody for special praise."—*Daily Mail.*

"The acting deserved a better play."—*Daily News.*

" ... Tommy ..."—*Morning Post.*

As Eustace read the papers he felt that his future was secure. True, *The Era*, careful never to miss a single performer, had yet to say, "Mr. Eustace Merrowby was capital as Tommy," and *The Stage*, "Tommy was capitally played by Mr. Eustace Merrowby"; but even without this he had become one of the Men who Count—one whose private life was of more interest to the public than that of any scientist, general or diplomat in the country.

Into Eustace Merrowby's subsequent career I cannot go at full length. It is perhaps as a member of the Garrick Club that he has attained his fullest development. All the good things of the Garrick which were not previously said by Sydney Smith may safely be put down to Eustace; and there is no doubt that he is the ringleader in all the subsequent practical jokes which have made the club famous. It was he who pinned to the back of an unpopular member of the committee a sheet of paper bearing the words

KICK ME

—and the occasion on which he drew the chair from beneath a certain eminent author as the latter was about to sit down is still referred to hilariously by the older members.

Finally, as a convincing proof of his greatness, let it be said that everybody has at least heard the name "Eustace Merrowby"—even though some may be under the impression that it is the trade-mark of a sauce; and that half the young ladies of Wandsworth Common and Winchmore Hill are in love with him. If this be not success, what is?

LI. THE COLLECTOR

When Peter Plimsoll, the Glue King, died, his parting advice to his sons to stick to the business was followed only by John, the elder. Adrian, the younger, had a soul above adhesion. He disposed of his share in the concern and settled down to follow the life of a gentleman of taste and culture and (more particularly) patron of the arts. He began in a modest way by collecting ink-pots. His range at first was catholic, and it was not until he had acquired a hundred and forty-seven ink-pots of various designs that he decided to make a specialty of historic ones. This decision was hastened by the discovery that one of Queen Elizabeth's inkstands—supposed (by the owner) to be the identical one with whose aid she wrote her last letter to Raleigh—was about to be put on the market. At some expense Adrian obtained an introduction, through a third party, to the owner, at more expense the owner obtained, through the same gentleman, an introduction to Adrian; and in less than a month the great Elizabeth Ink-pot was safely established in Adrian's house. It was the beginning of the "Plimsoll Collection."

This was twenty years ago. Let us to-day take a walk through the galleries of Mr. Adrian Plimsoll's charming residence which, as the world knows, overlooks the park. Any friend of mine is always welcome at Number Fifteen. We will start with the North Gallery; I fear that I shall only have time to point out a few of the choicest gems.

This is a Pontesiori sword of the thirteenth century—the only example of the master's art without any notches.

On the left is a Capricci comfit-box. If you have never heard of Capricci, you oughtn't to come to a house like this.

291

Here we have before us the historic de Montigny topaz. Ask your little boy to tell you about it.

In the East Gallery, of course, the chief treasure is the Santo di Santo amulet, described so minutely in his *Vindicia Veritatis* by John of Flanders. The original MS. of this book is in the South Gallery. You must glance at it when we get there. It will save you the trouble of ordering a copy from your library; they would be sure to keep you waiting....

With some such words as these I lead my friends round Number Fifteen. The many treasures in the private parts of the house I may not show, of course; the bathroom, for instance, in which hangs the finest collection of portraits of philatelists that Europe can boast. You must spend a night with Adrian to be admitted to their company; and as one of the elect, I can assure you that nothing can be more stimulating on a winter's morning than to catch the eye of Frisby Dranger, F.Ph.S., behind the taps as your head first emerges from the icy waters.

Adrian Plimsoll sat at breakfast, sipping his hot water and crumbling a dry biscuit. A light was in his eye, a flush upon his pallid countenance. He had just heard from a trusty agent that the Scutori breast-plate had been seen in Devonshire. His car was ready to take him to the station.

But alas! a disappointment awaited him. On close examination the breast-plate turned out to be a common Risoldo of inferior working. Adrian left the house in disgust and started on his seven-mile walk back to the station. To complete his misery a sudden storm came on.

Cursing alternately his agent and Risoldo, he made his way to a cottage and asked for shelter.

An old woman greeted him civilly and bade him come in.

"If I may just wait till the storm is over," said Adrian, and he sat down in her parlour and looked appraisingly (as was his habit) round the room. The grandfather clock in the corner was genuine, but he was beyond grandfather clocks. There was nothing else of any value; three china dogs and some odd trinkets on the chimney-piece; a print or two——

Stay! What was that behind the youngest dog?

"May I look at that old bracelet?" he asked, his voice trembling a little; and without waiting for permission he walked over and took up the circle of tarnished metal in his hands. As he examined it his colour came and went, his heart seemed to stop beating. With a tremendous effort he composed himself and returned to his chair.

It was the Emperor's Bracelet!

Of course you know the history of this most famous of all bracelets. Made by Spurius Quintus of Rome in 47 B.C., it was given by Cæsar to Cleopatra, who tried without success to dissolve it in vinegar. Returning to Rome by way of Antony it was worn at a minor conflagration by Nero, after which it was lost sight of for many centuries. It was eventually heard of during the reign of Canute (or Knut, as his admirers called him); and John is known to have lost it in the Wash, whence it was recovered a century afterwards. It must have travelled thence to France, for it was seen once in the possession of Louis XI; and from there to Spain, for Philip The Handsome presented it to Joanna on her wedding day.

Columbus took it to America, but fortunately brought it back again; Peter The Great threw it at an indifferent musician; on one of its later visits to England Pope wrote a couplet to it. And the most astonishing thing in its whole history was that now for more than a hundred years it had vanished completely. To turn up again in a little Devonshire cottage! Verily truth is stranger than fiction.

"That's rather a curious bracelet of yours," said Adrian casually. "My—er—wife has one just like it which she asked me to match. Is it an old friend, or would you care to sell it?"

"My mother gave it me," said the old woman, "and she had it from hers. I don't know no further than that. I didn't mean to sell it, but——"

"Quite right," said Adrian, "and after all, I can easily get another."

"But I won't say a bit of money wouldn't be useful. What would you think a fair price, Sir? Five shillings?"

Adrian's heart jumped. To get the Emperor's Bracelet for five shillings!

But the spirit of the collector rose up strong within him. He laughed kindly.

"My good woman," he said, "they turn out bracelets like that in Birmingham at two shillings apiece. And quite new. I'll give you tenpence."

"Make it one-and-sixpence," she pleaded. "Times are hard."

Adrian reflected. He was not, strictly speaking, impoverished. He could afford one-and-sixpence.

"One-and-tuppence," he said.

"No, no, one-and-sixpence," she repeated obstinately.

Adrian reflected again. After all, he could always sell it for ten thousand pounds, if the worst came to the worst.

"Well, well," he sighed, "one-and-sixpence let it be."

He counted out the money carefully. Then putting the precious bracelet in his pocket he rose to go.

Adrian has no relations living now. When he dies he proposes to leave the Plimsoll Collection to the nation, having, as far as he can foresee—no particular use for it in the next world. This is really very generous of him, and, no doubt, when the time comes, the papers will say so. But it is a pity that he cannot be appreciated properly in his lifetime. Personally I should like to see him knighted.

LII. THE STATESMAN

On a certain night in the middle of the season all London was gathered in Lady Marchpane's drawing-room; all London, that is, which was worth knowing—a qualification which accounted for the absence of several million people who had never heard of Lady Marchpane. In one corner of the room an Ambassador, with a few ribbons across his chest, could have been seen chatting to the latest American Duchess; in another corner one of our largest Advertisers was exchanging epigrams with a titled Newspaper Proprietor. Famous Generals rubbed shoulders with Post-Impressionist Artists; Financiers whispered sweet nothings to Breeders of prize Poms; even an Actor-Manager might have been seen accepting an apology from a Royalty who had jostled him.

"Hallo," said Algy Lascelles, catching sight of the dignified figure of Rupert Meryton in the crowd; "how's William?"

A rare smile lit up Rupert's distinguished features. He was Under-Secretary for Invasion Affairs, and "William" was Algy's pleasant way of referring to the Bill which he was now piloting through the House of Commons. It was a measure for doing something or other by means of a what d'you call it—I cannot be more precise without precipitating a European Conflict.

"I think we shall get it through," said Rupert calmly.

"Lady Marchpane was talking about it just now. She's rather interested, you know."

Rupert's lips closed about his mouth in a firm line. He looked over Algy's head into the crowd. "Oh!" he said coldly.

It was barely ten years ago that young Meryton, just down from Oxford, had startled the political world by capturing the important seat of Cricklewood (E.) for the Tariffadicals—as, to avoid plunging the country into Civil War, I must call them. This was at a by-election, and the Liberatives had immediately dissolved, only to come into power after the General Election with an increased majority. Through the years that followed, Rupert Meryton, by his pertinacity in asking the Invasion Secretary questions which had been answered by him on the previous day, and by his regard for the dignity of the House, as shown in his invariable comment, "Come, come—not quite the Gentleman," upon any display of bad manners opposite, established a clear right to a post in the subsequent Tariffadical Government. He had now been Under-Secretary for two years, and in this Bill his first real chance had come.

"Oh, there you are, Mr. Meryton," said a voice. "Come and talk to me a moment." With a nod to a couple of Archbishops Lady Marchpane led the way to a little gallery whither the crowd had not penetrated. Priceless Correggios, Tintorettos and G.K. Chestertons hung upon the walls, but it was not to show him these that she had come. Dropping into a wonderful old Chippendale chair, she motioned him to a Blundell-Maple opposite her, and looked at him with a curious smile.

"Well," she said, "about the Bill?"

Rupert's lips closed about his mouth in a firm line. (He was rather good at this.) Folding his arms, he gazed steadily into Lady Marchpane's still beautiful eyes.

"It will go through," he said. "Through all its stages," he added professionally.

"It must not go through," said Lady Marchpane gently.

Rupert could not repress a start, but he was master of himself again in a moment.

"I cannot add anything to my previous statement," he said.

"If it goes through," began Lady Marchpane——

"I must refer you," said Rupert, "to my answer of yesterday."

"Come, come, Mr. Meryton, what is the good of fencing with me? You know the position. Or shall I state it for you again?"

"I cannot believe you are serious."

"I am perfectly serious. There are reasons, financial reasons—and others, why I do not want this Bill to pass. In return for my silence upon a certain matter, you are going to prevent it passing. You know to what I refer. On the 4th of May last——"

"Stop!" cried Rupert hoarsely.

"On the 4th of May last," Lady Marchpane went on relentlessly, "you and I—in the absence of my husband abroad—had tea together at an A.B.C." (Rupert covered his face with his hands.) "I am no fonder of scandal than you are, but if you do not meet my wishes I shall certainly confess the truth to Marchpane."

"You will be ruined too!" said Rupert.

"My husband will forgive me and take me back." She paused significantly. "Will Marjorie Hale"—(Rupert covered his hands with his face)—"will the good Miss Hale forgive you? She is very strict, is she not? And rich? And rising young politicians want money more than scandal." She raised her head suddenly at the sound of footsteps. "Ah, Archbishop, I was just calling Mr. Meryton's attention to this wonderful Botticell"—(she looked at it more closely)—"this wonderful Dana Gibson. A beautiful piece of work, is it not?" The intruders passed on to the supper-room, and they were alone again.

"What am I to do?" said Rupert sullenly.

"The fate of the Bill is settled to-day week, when you make your big speech. You must speak against it. Confess frankly you were mistaken. It will be a close thing, anyhow. Your influence will turn the scale."

"It will ruin me politically."

"You will marry Marjorie Hale and be rich. No rich man is ever ruined politically. Or socially." She patted his hand gently. "You'll do it?"

He got up slowly. "You'll see next week," he said.

It is not meet that we should watch the unhappy Rupert through the long-drawn hours of the night, as he wrestled with the terrible problem. A moment's sudden madness on that May afternoon had brought him to the cross-roads. On the one hand, reputation, wealth, the girl that he loved; on the other, his own honour and—so, at least, he had said several times on the platform—the safety of England. He rose in the morning weary, but with his mind made up.

The Bill should go through!

Rupert Meryton was a speaker of a not unusual type. Although he provided the opinions himself, he always depended upon his secretary for the arguments with which to support them and the actual words in which to give them being. But on this occasion he felt that a special effort was required of him. He would show Lady Marchpane that the blackmail of yesterday had only roused him to a still greater sacrifice on behalf of his country. *He would write his own speech.*

On the fateful night the House was crowded. It seemed that all the guests at Lady Marchpane's a week before were in the Distinguished Strangers' Gallery or behind the Ladies' Grille. From the Press Gallery "Our Special Word-painter" looked down upon the statesmen beneath him, his eagle eye ready to detect on the moment the Angry Flush, the Wince, or the Sudden Paling of enemy, the Grim Smile or the Lofty Calm of friend.

The Rt. Hon. Rupert Meryton, Tariffadical Member for Cricklewood (E.) rose to his feet amidst cheers.

"Mr. Speaker," he said, "I rise—er—to-night, Sir—h'r'm, to—er——" So much of his speech I may give, but urgent State reasons compel me to withhold the rest. Were it ever known with which Bill the secret history that I have disclosed concerns itself, the Great Powers in an instant would be at each other's throats. But though I may not disclose the speech I can tell of its effect on the House. And its effect was curious. It was, in short, the exact opposite of what Rupert Meryton, that promising Under Secretary, had intended.

It was the first speech that he had ever prepared himself. Than Rupert there was no more dignified figure in the House of Commons; his honour was proof, as we have seen, against the most insidious temptations; yet, since one man cannot have all the virtues, he was distinctly stupid. It would have been a hopeless speech anyhow; but, to make matters worse, he had, in the most important part of it, attempted irony. And at the beginning of the ironical passage even the Tariffadical word-painters had to confess that it was their own stalwarts who "suddenly paled."

As Lady Marchpane had said, it was bound to be a close thing. The Liberatives and the Unialists, of course, were solid against the Bill, but there was also something of a cave in the Tariffadical Party. It was bound to be a close thing, and Rupert's speech just made the difference. When he sat down the waverers and doubters had made up their minds.

The Bill was defeated.

That the Tariffadicals should resign was natural; perhaps it was equally natural that Rupert's secretary should resign too. He said that his reputation would be gone if Rupert made any more speeches on his own, and that he wasn't going to risk it. Without his secretary Rupert was lost at the General Election which followed. Fortunately he had a grateful friend in Lady Marchpane. She exerted her influence with the Liberatives, and got him an appointment as Governor of the Stickjaw Islands. Here, with his beautiful and rich wife, Sir Rupert Meryton maintains a regal state, and upon his name no breath of scandal rests. Indeed his only trouble so far has been with the Stickjaw language—a difficult language, but one which, perhaps fortunately, does not lend itself to irony.

LIII. THE MAGNATE

It was in October, 19—, that the word "Zinc" first began to be heard in financial circles. City men, pushing their dominoes regretfully away, and murmuring "Zinc" in apologetic tones, were back in their offices by three o'clock, forgetting in their haste to leave the usual twopence under the cup for the waitress. Clubmen, glancing at the tape on their way to the smoking-room, said to their neighbours, "Zinc's moved a point, I see," before covering themselves up with the *Times*. In the trains, returning husbands asked each other loudly, "What's all this about zinc?"—all save the very innocent ones, who whispered, "I say, what *is* zinc exactly?" The music-halls took it up. No sooner had the word "Zinc" left the lips of an acknowledged comedian than the house was in roars of laughter. The furore at the Collodium when Octavius Octo, in his world-famous part of the landlady of a boarding-house, remarked, "I know why my ole man's so late. 'E's buying zinc," is still remembered in the bars round Piccadilly.

To explain it properly it will be necessary (my readers will be alarmed to hear) to go back some thirty years. This, as a simple calculation shows, takes us to June, 18—. It was in June, 18—, that Felix Moses, a stout young man of attractive appearance (if you care for that style), took his courage in both hands, and told Phyllida Sloan that he was worth ten thousand a year and was changing his name to Mountenay. Miss Sloan, seeing that it was the beginning of a proposal, said hastily that she was changing hers to Abraham.

"You're marrying Leo Abraham?" asked Felix in amazement. "Ah!" A gust of jealousy swept over him. He licked his lips. There was a dangerous look in his eyes—a look that was destined in after days to make Emperors and rival financiers quail. "Ah!" he said softly. "Leo Abraham! I shall not forget!"

And now it will be necessary (my readers will be relieved to learn) to jump forward some thirty years. This obviously takes us to September, 19—. Let us, on this fine September morning, take a peep into "No.——, Throgneedle Street, E. C.," and see how the business of the mother city is carried on.

On the fourth floor we come to the sanctum of the great man himself. "Mr. Felix Mountenay—No admittance," is painted upon the outer door. It is a name which is known and feared all over Europe. Mr. Mountenay's private detective stands on one side of the door; on the other side is Mr. Mountenay's private wolfhound. Murmuring the word, "Press," however, we pass hastily through, and find ourselves before Mr. Mountenay himself. Mr. Mountenay is at work; let us watch him through a typical five minutes.

For a moment he stands meditating in the middle of the room. Kings are tottering on their thrones. Empires hang upon his nod. What will he decide? Suddenly he blows a cloud of smoke from his cigar, and rushes to the telephone.

"Hallo! Is that you, Jones?... What are
Margarine *Prefs*. at?... *What?* ... No, Margarine Prefs. idiot.... Ah!
Then sell. Keep on selling till I tell you to stop.... Yes."

He hangs up the receiver. For two minutes he paces the room, smoking rapidly. He stops a moment ... but it is only to remove his cigar-band, which is in danger of burning. Then he resumes his pacings. Another minute goes rapidly by. He rushes to the telephone again.

"Hallo! Is that you, Jones?... What are Margarine Prefs. down to now?... Ah! Then buy. Keep on buying.... Yes."

He hangs up the receiver. By this master-stroke he has made a quarter of a million. It may seem to you or me an easy way of doing it. Ah, but what, we must ask ourselves, of the great brain that conceived the idea, the foresight which told the exact moment when to put it into action, the cool courage which seized the moment— what of the grasp of affairs, the knowledge of men? Ah! Can we grudge it him, that he earns a quarter of a million more quickly than we do?

Yet Mr. Felix Mountenay is not happy. When we have brought off a coup for a hundred thousand even, we smile gaily. Mr. Mountenay did not smile. Fiercely he bit another inch off his cigar and muttered to himself.

The words were "Leo Abraham! Wait!"

This is positively the last row of stars. Let us take advantage of them to jump forward another month. It was October 1st, 19—. (If that was a Sunday, then it was October 2nd. Anyhow, it was October.)

Mr. Felix Mountenay was sleeping in his office. For once that iron brain relaxed. He had made a little over three million in the last month and the strain was too much for him. But a knock at the door restored him instantly to his own cool self.

"I beg your pardon, Sir," said his secretary, "but somebody is selling zinc."

The word "Zinc" touched a chord in Mr. Mountenay's brain which had lain dormant for years. Zinc! Why did zinc remind him of Leo Abraham?

"Fetch the Encyclopædia Britannica, quick!" he cried.

The secretary, a man of herculean build, returned with some of it. With the luck which proverbially attends rich men Mr. Mountenay picked up the "Z" volume at once. As he read the Zinc article it all came back to him. Leo Abraham had owned an empty zinc-mine! Was his enemy in his clutches at last?

"Buy!" he said briefly.

In a fortnight the secretary had returned.

"Well," said Mr. Mountenay, "have you bought all the zinc that there is?"

"Yes, Sir," said the Secretary. "And a lot that there isn't," he added.

"Good!" He paused a moment. "When Mr. Leo Abraham calls," he added grimly, "show him up at once."

It was a month later that a haggard man climbed the stairs of No.——, Throgneedle Street, and was shown into Mr. Mountenay's room.

"Well," said the financier softly, "what can I do for you?"

"I want some zinc," said Leo Abergavenny.

"Zinc," said Mr. Mountenay with a smile, "is a million pounds a ton. Or an acre, or a gallon, or however you prefer to buy it," he added humorously.

Leo went white.

"You wish to ruin me?"

"I do. A promise I made to your wife some years ago."

"My wife?" cried Leo. "What do you mean? I'm not married."

It was Mr. Mountenay's turn to go white. He went it.

"Not married? But Miss Sloan——"

Mr. Leo Abergavenny sat down and mopped his face.

"I don't know what you mean," he said. "I asked Miss Sloan to marry me, and told her I was changing my name to Abergavenny. And she said that she was changing hers to Moses. Naturally, I thought——"

"Stop!" cried Mr. Mountenay. He sat down heavily. Something seemed to have gone out of his life; in a moment the world was empty. He looked up at his old rival, and forced a laugh.

"Well, well," he said, "she deceived us both. Let us drink to our lucky escape." He rang the bell.

"And then," he said in a purring voice, "we can have a little talk about zinc. After all, business is still business."

LIV. THE ADVENTURER

Lionel Norwood, from his earliest days, had been marked out for a life of crime. When quite a child he was discovered by his nurse killing flies on the window-pane. This was before the character of the house-fly had become a matter of common talk among scientists, and Lionel (like all great men, a little before his time) had pleaded hygiene in vain. He was smacked hastily and bundled off to a preparatory school, where his aptitude for smuggling sweets would have lost him many a half-holiday had not his services been required at outside-left in the hockey eleven. With some difficulty he managed to pass into Eton, and three years later—with, one would imagine, still more difficulty—managed to get superannuated. At Cambridge he went down-hill rapidly. He would think nothing of smoking a cigar in academical costume, and on at least one occasion he drove a dogcart on Sunday. No wonder that he was requested, early in his second year, to give up his struggle with the Little-go and betake himself back to London.

London is always glad to welcome such people as Lionel Norwood. In no other city is it so simple for a man of easy conscience to earn a living by his wits. If Lionel ever had any scruples (which, after a perusal of the above account of his early days, it may be permitted one to doubt) they were removed by an accident to his solicitor, who was run over in the Argentine on the very day that he arrived there with what was left of Lionel's money. Reduced suddenly to poverty, Norwood had no choice but to enter upon a life of crime.

Except, perhaps, that he used slightly less hair-oil than most, he seemed just the ordinary man about town as he sat in his dressing-gown one fine summer morning and smoked a cigarette. His rooms were furnished quietly and in the best of taste. No signs of his nefarious profession showed themselves to the casual visitor. The appealing letters from the Princess whom he was blackmailing, the wire apparatus which shot the two of spades down his sleeve during the coon-can nights at the club, the thimble and pea with which he had performed the three-card trick so successfully at Epsom last week—all these were hidden away from the common gaze. It was a young gentleman of fashion who lounged in his chair and toyed with a priceless straight-cut.

There was a tap at the door, and Masters, his confidential valet, came in.

"Well," said Lionel, "have you looked through the post?"

"Yes, Sir," said the man. "There's the usual cheque from Her Highness, a request for more time from the lady in Tite Street with twopence to pay on the envelope, and banknotes from the Professor as expected. The young gentleman of Hill Street has gone abroad suddenly, Sir."

"Ah!" said Lionel, with a sudden frown. "I suppose you'd better cross him off our list, Masters."

"Yes, Sir. I had ventured to do so, Sir. I think that's all, except that Mr. Snooks is glad to accept your kind invitation to dinner and bridge to-night. Will you wear the hair-spring coat, Sir, or the metal clip?"

Lionel made no answer. He sat plunged in thought. When he spoke it was about another matter.

"Masters," he said, "I have found out Lord Fairlie's secret at last. I shall go to see him this afternoon."

"Yes, Sir. Will you wear your revolver, Sir, as it's a first call?"

"I think so. If this comes off, Masters, it will make our fortune."

"I hope so, I'm sure, Sir." Masters placed the whisky within reach and left the room silently.

Alone, Lionel picked up his paper and turned to the Agony Column.

As everybody knows, the Agony Column of a daily paper is not actually so domestic as it seems. When "Mother" apparently says to "Floss," "Come home at once. Father gone away for week. Bert and Sid longing to see you," what is really happening is that Barney Hoker is telling Jud Batson to meet him outside the Duke of Westminster's little place at 3 a.m. precisely on Tuesday morning, not forgetting to bring his jemmy and a dark lantern with him. And Floss's announcement next day, "Coming home with George," is Jud's way of saying that he will turn up all right, and half thinks of bringing his automatic pistol with him too, in case of accidents.

In this language—which, of course, takes some little learning—Lionel Norwood had long been an expert. The advertisement which he was now reading was unusually elaborate:

"Lost, in a taxi between Baker Street and Shepherd's Bush, a gold-mounted umbrella with initials 'J. P.' on it. If Ellen will return to her father immediately all will be forgiven. White spot on foreleg. Mother very anxious and desires to return thanks for kind enquiries. Answers to the name of Ponto. *Bis dat qui cito dat.*"

What did it mean? For Lionel it had no secrets. He was reading the revelation by one of his agents of the skeleton in Lord Fairlie's cupboard!

Lord Fairlie was one of the most distinguished members of the Cabinet. His vein of high seriousness, his lofty demeanour, the sincerity of his manner, endeared him not only to his own party, but even (astounding as it may seem) to a few high-minded men upon the other side, who admitted, in moments of expansion which they probably regretted afterwards, that he might, after all, be as devoted to his country as they were. For years now his life had been without blemish. It was impossible to believe that even in his youth he could have sown any wild oats; terrible to think that these wild oats might now be coming home to roost.

"What do you require of me?" he said courteously to Lionel, as the latter was shown into his study.

Lionel went to the point at once.

"I am here, my lord," he said, "on business. In the course of my ordinary avocations"—the parliamentary atmosphere seemed to be affecting his language—"I ascertained a certain secret in your past life which, if it were revealed, might conceivably have a not undamaging effect upon your career. For my silence in this matter I must demand a sum of fifty thousand pounds."

Lord Fairlie had grown paler and paler as this speech proceeded.

"What have you discovered?" he whispered. Alas! he knew only too well what the damning answer would be.

"*Twenty years ago*," said Lionel, "*you wrote a humorous book.*"

Lord Fairlie gave a strangled cry. His keen mind recognised in a flash what a hold this knowledge would give his enemies. *Shafts of Folly*, his book had been called. Already he saw the leading articles of the future:

"We confess ourselves somewhat at a loss to know whether Lord Fairlie's speech at Plymouth yesterday was intended as a supplement to his earlier work, *Shafts of Folly*, or as a serious offering to a nation impatient of levity in such a crisis...."

"The Cabinet's jester, in whom twenty years ago the country lost an excellent clown without gaining a statesman, was in great form last night...."

"Lord Fairlie has amused us in the past with his clever little parodies; he may amuse us in the future; but as a statesman we can only view him with disgust...."

"Well?" said Lionel at last. "I think your lordship is wise enough to understand. The discovery of a sense of humour in a man of your eminence——"

But Lord Fairlie was already writing out the cheque.

LV. THE EXPLORER

As the evening wore on—and one young man after another asked Jocelyn Montrevor if she were going to Ascot, what? or to Henley, what? or what? she wondered more and more if this were all that life would ever hold for her. Would she never meet a man, a real man who had done something? These boys around her were very pleasant, she admitted to herself; very useful, indeed, she added, as one approached her with some refreshment; but they were only boys.

"Here you are," said Freddy, handing her an ice in three colours. "I've had it made specially cold for you. They only had the green, pink and yellow jerseys left; I hope you don't mind. The green part is arsenic, I believe. If you don't want the wafer I'll take it home and put it between the sashes of my bedroom window. The rattling kept me awake all last night. That's why I'm looking so ill, by-the-way."

Jocelyn smiled kindly and went on with her ice.

"That reminds me," Freddy went on, "we've got a nut here to-night. The genuine thing. None of your society Barcelonas or suburban Filberts. One of the real Cob family; the driving-from-the-sixth-tee, inset-on-the-right, and New-Year's-message-to-the-country touch. In short, a celebrity."

"Who?" asked Jocelyn eagerly. Perhaps here was a man.

"Worrall Brice, the explorer. Don't say you haven't heard of him or Aunt Alice will cry."

Heard of him? Of course she had heard of him. Who hadn't?

Worrall Brice's adventures in distant parts of the empire would have filled a book—had, in fact, already filled three. A glance at his flat in

St. James' Street gave you some idea of the adventures he had been through. Here were the polished spurs of his companion in the famous ride through Australia from south to north—all that had been left by the cannibals of the Wogga-Wogga River after their banquet. Here was the poisoned arrow which, by the merciful intervention of Providence, just missed Worrall and pierced the heart of one of his black attendants, the post-mortem happily revealing the presence of a new and interesting poison. Here, again, was the rope with which he was hanged by mistake as a spy in South America—a mistake which would certainly have had fatal results if he had not had the presence of mind to hold his breath during the performance. In yet another corner you might see his favourite mascot, a tooth of the shark which bit him off the coast of China. Spears, knives and guns lined the walls; every inch of the floor was covered by skins. His flat was typical of the man—a man who had done things.

"Introduce him to me," commanded Jocelyn. "Where is he?"

She looked up suddenly and saw him entering the ballroom. He was of commanding height and his face was the face of the man who has been exposed to the forces of Nature. The wind, the waves, the sun, the mosquito had set their mark upon him. Down one side of his cheek was a newly healed scar, a scratch from a hippopotamus in its last death-struggle. A legacy from a bison seared his brow.

He walked with the soft, easy tread of the python, or the Pathan, or some animal with a "pth" in it. Probably I mean the panther. He bore himself confidently, and his mouth was a trap from which no superfluous word escaped. He was the strong, silent man of Jocelyn's dreams.

"Mr. Worrall Brice, Miss Montrevor," said Freddy, and left them.

Worrall Brice bowed and stood beside her with folded arms, his gaze fixed above her head.

"I shall not expect you to dance," said Jocelyn, with a confidential smile which implied that he and she were above such frivolities. As a matter of fact, he could have taught her the Wogga-Wogga one-step, the Bimbo, the Kiyi, the Ju-bu, the Head-hunter's Hug and many other cannibalistic steps which, later on, were to become the rage of London and the basis of a revue.

"I have often imagined you as you kept watch over your camp," she went on, "and I have seemed myself to hear the savages and lions roaring outside the circle of fire, what time in the swamps the crocodiles were barking."

"Yes," he said.

"It must be a wonderful life."

"Yes."

"If I were a man I should want to lead such a life; to get away from all this," and she waved her hand round the room, "back to Nature. To know that I could not eat until I had first killed my dinner; that I could not live unless I slew the enemy! That must be fine!"

"Yes," said Worrall.

"I can't get Freddy to see it. He is quite content to have shot a few grouse ... and once to have wounded a beater. There must be more in life than that."

"Yes."

"I suppose I am elemental. Beneath the veneer of civilisation I am a savage. To wake up with the war-cry of the enemy in my ears, to sleep with the—er—barking of the crocodile in my dreams, that is life!"

Worrall Brice tugged at his moustache and gazed into space over her head. Then he spoke.

"Crocodiles don't bark," he said.

Jocelyn looked at him in astonishment. "But in your book, *Through Trackless Paths*!" she cried, "I know it almost by heart. It was you who taught me. What are the beautiful words? 'On the banks of the sleepy river two great crocodiles were barking.'"

"Not 'barking,'" said Worrall. "'Basking.' It was a misprint."

"Oh!" said Jocelyn. She had a moment's awful memory of all the occasions when she had insisted that crocodiles barked. There had been a particularly fierce argument with Meta Richards, who had refused to weigh even the printed word of Worrall Brice against the silence of the Reptile House on her last visit to the Zoo.

"Well," smiled Jocelyn, "you must teach me about these things. Will you come and see me?"

"Yes," said Worrall. He rather liked to stand and gaze into the distance while pretty women talked to him. And Jocelyn was very pretty.

"We live in South Kensington. Come on Sunday, won't you? 99, Peele Crescent."

"Yes," said Worrall.

On Sunday Jocelyn waited eagerly for him in the drawing-room of Peele Crescent. Her father was asleep in the library, her mother was dead; so she would have the great man to herself for an afternoon. Later she would have him for always, for she meant to marry him. And when they were married she was not so sure that they would live with the noise of the crocodile barking or coughing, or whatever it did, in their ears. She saw herself in that little house in Green Street, with the noise of motor-horns and taxi-whistles to soothe her to sleep.

Yet what a man he was! What had he said to her? She went over all his words.... They were not many.

At six o'clock she was still waiting in the drawing-room at Peele Crescent....

At six-thirty Worrall Brice had got as far as Peele Place....

At six-forty-five he was back in Peele Square again....

At seven o'clock, just as he was giving himself up for lost, he met a taxi and returned to St. James' Street. He was a great Traveller, but South Kensington had been too much for him.

Next week he went back unmarried to the jungle. It was the narrowest escape he had had.

LVI. THE NEWSPAPER PROPRIETOR

The great Hector Strong, lord of journalism and swayer of empires, paced the floor of his luxurious apartment with bowed head, his corrugated countenance furrowed with lines of anxiety. He had just returned from a lunch with all his favourite advertisers ... but it was not this which troubled him. He was thinking out a new policy for *The Daily Vane*.

Suddenly he remembered something. Coming up to town in his third motor, he had glanced through the nineteen periodicals which his house had published that morning, and in one case had noted matter for serious criticism. This was obviously the first business he must deal with.

He seated himself at his desk and pushed the bell marked "38." Instantly a footman presented himself with a tray of sandwiches.

"What do you want?" said Strong coldly.

"You rang for me, Sir," replied the trembling menial.

"Go away," said Strong. Recognising magnanimously, however, that the mistake was his own, he pressed bell "28." In another moment the editor of *Sloppy Chunks* was before him.

"In to-day's number," said Strong, as he toyed with a blue pencil, "you apologise for a mistake in last week's number." He waited sternly.

"It was a very bad mistake, Sir, I'm afraid. We did a great injustice to——"

"You know my rule," said Strong. "The mistake of last week I could have overlooked. The apology of this week is a more serious matter. You will ask for a month's salary on your way out." He pressed a button and the editor disappeared through the trap-door.

Alone again, Hector Strong thought keenly for a moment. Then he pressed bell "38." Instantly a footman presented himself with a tray of sandwiches.

"What do you mean by this?" roared Strong, his iron self-control for a moment giving way.

"I b-beg your pardon, Sir," stammered the man. "I th-thought——"

"Get out!" As the footman retired, Strong passed his hand across his forehead. "My memory is bad to-day," he murmured, and pushed bell "48."

A tall, thin man entered.

"Ah, good afternoon, Mr. Brownlow," said the Proprietor. He toyed with his blue pencil. "Let me see, which of our papers are under your charge at the moment?"

Mr. Brownlow reflected.

"Just now," he said, "I am editing *Snippety Snips*, *The Whoop*, *The Girls' Own Aunt*, *Parings*, *The Sunday Sermon*, *Slosh* and *Back Chat*."

"Ah! Well, I want you to take on *Sloppy Chunks*, too, for a little while. Mr. Symes has had to leave us."

"Yes, Sir." Mr. Brownlow bowed and moved to the door.

"By the way," Strong said, "your last number of *Slosh* was very good. Very good indeed. I congratulate you. Good day."

Left alone, Hector Strong, lord of journalism and swayer of empires, resumed his pacings. His two mistakes with the bell told him that he was distinctly not himself this afternoon. Was it only the need of a new policy for *The Vane* which troubled him? Or was it——

Could it be Lady Dorothy?

Lady Dorothy Neal was something of an enigma to Hector Strong. He was making more than a million pounds a year, and yet she did not want to marry him. Sometimes he wondered if the woman were quite sane. Yet, mad or sane, he loved her.

A secretary knocked and entered. He waited submissively for half-an-hour until the Proprietor looked up.

"Well?"

"Lady Dorothy Neal would like to see you for a moment, Sir."

"Show her in."

Lady Dorothy came in brightly.

"What nice-looking men you have here," she said. "Who is the one in the blue waistcoat? He has curly hair."

"You didn't come to talk about *him*?" said Hector reproachfully.

"I didn't come to talk *to* him really, but if you keep me waiting half-an-hour—— Why, what are you doing?"

Strong looked up from the note he was writing. The tender lines had gone from his face, and he had become the stern man of action again.

"I am giving instructions that the services of my commissionaire, hall-boy, and fifth secretary will no longer be required."

"Don't do that," pleaded Dorothy.

Strong tore up the note and turned to her. "What do you want of me?" he asked.

She blushed and looked down. "I—I have written a—a play," she faltered.

He smiled indulgently. He did not write plays himself but he knew that other people did.

"When does it come off?" he asked.

"The manager says it will have to at the end of the week. It came *on* a week ago."

"Well," he smiled, "if people don't want to go, I can't make them."

"Yes you can," she said boldly.

He gave a start. His brain working at lightning speed saw the possibilities in an instant. At one stroke he could win Lady Dorothy's gratitude, provide *The Daily Vane* with a temporary policy and give a convincing exhibition of the power of his press.

"Oh, Mr. Strong——"

"Hector," he whispered. As he rose from his desk to go to her, he accidentally pressed the button of the trap-door. The next moment he was alone.

"That the British public is always ready to welcome the advent of a clean and wholesome home-grown play is shown by the startling success of *Christina's Mistake*, which is attracting such crowds to The King's every night." So wrote *The Daily Vane*, and continued in the same strain for a column.

"Clubland is keenly exercised," wrote *The Evening Vane*, "over a problem of etiquette which arises in the Second Act of *Christina's Mistake*, the great autumn success at The King's Theatre. The point is shortly this. Should a woman ..." And so on.

"A pretty story is going the rounds," said *Slosh*, "anent that charming little lady, Estelle Rito, who plays the part of a governess in *Christina's Mistake*, for which ("Manager" Barodo informs me) advance booking up to Christmas has already been taken. It seems that Miss Rito when shopping in the purlieus of Bond Street ..."

Sloppy Chunks had a joke which set all the world laughing. It was called

"BETWEEN THE ACTS."

Flossie. Who's the lady in the box with Mr. Johnson?

Gussie. Hush! It's his wife!

And Flossie giggled so much that she could hardly listen to the last Act of *Christina's Mistake*, which she had been looking forward to for weeks!

The *Sunday Sermon* offered free tickets to a hundred unmarried suburban girls, to which class *Christina's Mistake* might be supposed to make a special religious appeal. But they had to collect coupons first for *The Sunday Sermon*.

And finally *The Times* of two months later, said:

"A marriage has been arranged between Lady Dorothy Neal, daughter of the Earl of Skye, and the Hon. Geoffrey Bollinger."

Than a successful revenge nothing is sweeter in life. Hector Strong was not the man to spare any one who had done him an injury. Yet I think his method of revenging himself upon Lady Dorothy savoured of the diabolical. He printed a photograph of her in *The Daily Picture Gallery*. It was headed "The Beautiful Lady Dorothy Neal."

THE END

www.ingramcontent.com/pod-product-compliance
Lightning Source LLC
Chambersburg PA
CBHW070628290526
45790CB00001B/39

* 9 7 8 1 4 8 1 8 4 7 7 6 6 *